A CAVER'S

CAV
SOUTH WALES

Tim Stratford

Photographs by Tony Baker

CORDEE - LEICESTER

First Edition 1978

Second Edition 1982

Third Edition 1986

This Edition 1995

Front Cover photograph: Ogof Ffynnon Ddu 1

Rear cover photograph: Neil Weymouth in Otter Hole

ISBN 1 871890 03 9

British Library Cataloguing in Publication Data
A catalogue record for this book is available from the British Library

All trade enquiries to:
Cordee, 3a De Montfort Street, Leicester LE1 7HD

This book is available from all specialist equipment shops and major booksellers. It can, along with all the maps mentioned in the text, be obtained direct from the publishers. Please write for a copy of our comprehensive stocklist of outdoor recreation and travel books and maps.

CORDEE
3a De Montfort Street, Leicester LE1 7HD

Contents

Surveys

Introduction

It is now nine years since the last edition of this guide was published and seventeen years since the original edition in 1978. During that time there has been a very dramatic upturn in Welsh caving and this is reflected by the number of caves described in this latest edition compared with that of 1978. This fourth edition contains descriptions of 137 major caves against only 90 in the '78 edition. However, that is only part of the picture as a significant number of the new caves described are very extensive systems. The latest discovery for example, Ogof Draenen, is over 26 km and still going. If we compare the total length of passages described in the '78 edition (121 km) with that of this edition (234 km), the difference is quite dramatic.

South Wales therefore is now established as one of the most important caving regions in the British Isles, second only, perhaps, to the Yorkshire Dales. Caves in South Wales contain many unique features and much has been done to conserve and protect them. It is important that we not only keep up the momentum of exploration and new discoveries, but also continue to take conservation measures to protect our caves for future generations. It is up to ordinary cavers like you and me. Our record in South Wales is very good, but maybe we could do even better.

Tim Stratford

Acknowledgements

The completion of this guide would not have been possible without the help and support of cavers active in South Wales. It is impossible to thank everyone personally but in particular I would like to thank the following for their help in bringing the guide up to date :- Bill Gascoigne, Andy Ward, Alistair Garman, Duncan Price, Tim Gilson, Mike Green, Andy Clark, Liam Kealy, Jeff Hill, Keith Jones, Gus Horsley, Ashley   Dickenson, and John Hutchinson.

I am also indebted to the Royal Forest of Dean C.C., Chelsea S.S., Isca C.C, Westminster S.S., Swindon S.S., Grwp Ogofeidd Craig-a-Ffynnon, Brymawr C.C., Tefli Valley C.G., Llanelly Diggers, and Paul Taylor for the use of their surveys.

If I have forgotten to mention someone, please forgive me. I am nevertheless grateful for your help.

The Major Caves of South Wales

		length
Ogof Ffynnon Ddu	Area 7	50,000 m
Agen Allwedd	Area 3	32,000 m
Ogof Draenen	Area 2	28,000 m +
Ogof y Daren Cilau	Area 3	26,000 m +
Dan yr Ogof	Area 7	15,500 m
Ogof Craig-a-Ffynnon	Area 2	12,800 m
Slaughter Stream Cave	Area 1	12,000 m
Little Neath River Cave	Area 6	7,855 m
Ogof Carno	Area 2	7,000 m
Otter Hole	Area 1	3,352 m
Porth-yr-Ogof	Area 6	2,220 m
Tunnel Cave	Area 7	2,135 m
Llanelly Quarry Pot	Area 2	1,705 m
Redhouse Swallet	Area 1	1,615 m
Tooth Cave	Area 9	1,525 m

Advice to Beginners

The best advice to anyone who is contemplating taking up caving is to JOIN A REPUTABLE CLUB. There are many clubs active in South Wales and a list of some of them appears below.

Caving can be potentially dangerous but it can also be relatively safe. By joining a club and drawing on the experience of others the beginner can avoid the hazards which might otherwise lead him to serious injury or even worse. For some, caving is basically common sense, but for most people the best way to learn is with experienced cavers under actual caving conditions. No amount of bookwork can ever replace practical experience.

There are many other advantages to joining a club. The tackle required to visit some caves can run into hundreds of pounds and as most clubs have a store of tackle available for use by members this can save the potential caver a great deal of expense. Some clubs also have their own accommodation available and this can be a great asset especially in Wales which is usually very wet and cold in winter. Most clubs have a library which can be a useful source of information and many produce their own newsletter to keep members in touch with what's going on. Membership fees are often quite low and represent good value for money. It therefore makes good sense to JOIN A CLUB.

Clubs active or formerly active in South Wales

BCC	Brynmawr Caving Club
BNSSS	British Nylon Spinners Speleological Society
BUSS	Birmingham University Speleological Society
CCC	Croydon Caving Club
CCC	Cwmbran Caving Club
CDG	Cave Diving Group
CSS	Chelsea Speleological Society
GOCAF	Grwp Ogofeidd Craig-a-Ffynnon
GSS	Gloucester Speleological Society
HCC	Hereford Caving Club

ICC	Isca Caving Club
MCC	Morgannwg Caving Club
OUCC	Oxford University Caving Club
RFDCC	Royal Forest of Dean Caving Club
SSS	Swindon Speleological Society
SUSS	Sheffield University Speleological Society
SVCC	Severn Valley Caving Club
SWCC	South Wales Caving Club
TSU	Technical Speleological Unit
TVCG	Tefli Valley Caving Group
UBSS	University of Bristol Speleological Society
WSG	Westminster Speleological Group

There are also many other Welsh and English clubs which cave frequently in South Wales. Up to date addresses for any of the above or for clubs not listed can be obtained from the Secretary of the Cambrian Caving Council (see address at the bottom of the following section).

Cambrian Caving Council

(Cyngor Ogofeydd Cymreig)
The Cambrian Caving Council is an association of caving clubs and organisations. It is represented nationally on the Sports Council for Wales, both in the Welsh Sports and Games Association and the Outdoor Pursuits Group and regionally on the National Caving Association in the Executive and Special Committees on Conservation and Access, Novice Training and Equipment. Its membership is steadily increasing and now stands at 35 clubs. A club is eligible for membership if it is established in the region or has major interests there. It requires the sponsorship of one one-year old member-club in applying for membership.
The aims and objectives of the Cambrian Caving Council are:
(a) To encourage the exchange of information between clubs and with other regional and national bodies.
(b) To safeguard the interests of caving clubs.
(c) To maintain friendly relations with, and foster the spirit of co-operation between, similar and associated bodies with a view to promoting and achieving objects of mutual interest.
(d) To encourage the recording of information on sites of speleological interest in Wales and the Marches, in the Cambrian Cave Registry or a similar body.
(e) To encourage conservation.
(f) To support clubs in obtaining, maintaining and improving access arrangements for the benefit of all clubs.
(g) To establish and maintain good relations with non-caving bodies.

For further information contact the Hon. Sec., Frank Baguley, The White Lion, Ynys Uchaf, Ystradgynlais, Nr. Swansea, SA9 1RW.

Cambrian Cave Registry

The Registry collects information on Welsh caves and sites of speleological interest. The information is readily available to all cavers. Each area is covered by a different registrar who voluntarily collects and checks the information before feeding it into the central Register. The Registry has been an enormous help to the author in compiling this book.

"For further information contact Bill Gascoine, 18 Groveside Villas, Pontnewynydd, Pontypool, Gwent NP4 6SZ."

Conservation

Welsh caves are remarkably well preserved and clean and it is the responsibility of all cavers to see that they remain so.

DO NOT LEAVE LITTER inside our outside the cave. If you see litter within a caver please pick it up and take it out with you.

IF YOU SEE SOMEONE DUMPING REFUSE in a cave entrance report it to an organisation like the Cambrian Caving Council or do something about it yourself.

DO NOT DUMP CARBIDE in or outside of a cave. This can seriously upset cave life as well as being unsightly. If you use a carbide lamp take a container with you and take away the spent material.

NEVER BREAK OFF OR REMOVE FORMATIONS. Remember they look much better in the natural beauty of a cave than they do on a mantelpiece.

DO NOT TOUCH FORMATIONS, WRITE ON THE WALLS OR DISTURB CAVE LIFE. The damage is usually permanent.

There is an old saying which says "Take nothing but photographs, leave nothing but footprints".

Access

Access to caves in Wales provides few problems but remember that the land always belongs to someone. Do not upset landowners and observe the country code. This will ensure easy access for future generations of cavers as well as ourselves. Where access regulations do apply, observe them carefully.

Cave Rescue

In the event of an accident requiring the necessity to call for cave rescue the following procedure should be followed:

(1) Find the nearest telephone, dial 999 and ask for the Police.
(2) When connected ask for Cave Rescue.
(3) Give your name, telephone number and location.
(4) Remain at the phone until you are contacted by a Cave Rescue Warden.
(5) Wait until the rescue team arrives.

Note: The Police and Rescue Warden will want the most accurate information possible. Please be clear and precise, it can save a great deal of time later. Those remaining in the cave with the injured person should try to keep him as warm as possible and administer basic first aid if necessary.

How to use this Guide

The book is divided into nine area sections. Each contains an area map, descriptions of the main caves and a list of lesser caves and sites of speleological interest. Each description of the main caves includes a Grid Reference and Ordnance Survey Map Nos., Length and/or Depth, details of Location and Access where appropriate, a Description of the Cave, details of Tackle required and a brief History of Exploration and details of any Survey. The Ordnance Survey Maps quoted are the 1:50 000 sheet and the larger scale 1:25 000. Where appropriate the 1:25 000 Outdoor Leisure Series maps are quoted as these are generally more easily obtainable than the ordinary 1:25 000 sheet. There should be few problems in finding a cave if the details of Location are used in conjunction with the appropriate map.

The Description of the Cave gives details of the main route with information or side passages etc. in italics. Diver information is in small capital type.

Grading System

Although the grading of caves is generally disliked by experienced cavers, especially in Wales, the author feels that some kind of guide is essential. The grading system is intended as a guide to less experienced cavers to give them some idea of the level of difficulty of the cave. As every individual varies in the level of his ability the grading system can only be a loose guide. The caves are graded from 1 to 5 as follows:

GRADE 1 Easy Cave with no real difficulties or dangers.
GRADE 2 Easy Cave with minor difficulties.
GRADE 3 Moderate Cave with some difficulties but no real hazards.
GRADE 4 Difficult Cave with considerable difficulties and/or hazards requiring a certain amount of skill and/or stamina.
GRADE 5 Severe Cave with serious difficulties and/or hazards which requires a considerable amount of skill and/or stamina.

Where no grade is given it means that the cave is only accessible to divers or that access is forbidden or dangerous.

SOUTHEAST WALES AND THE FOREST OF DEAN

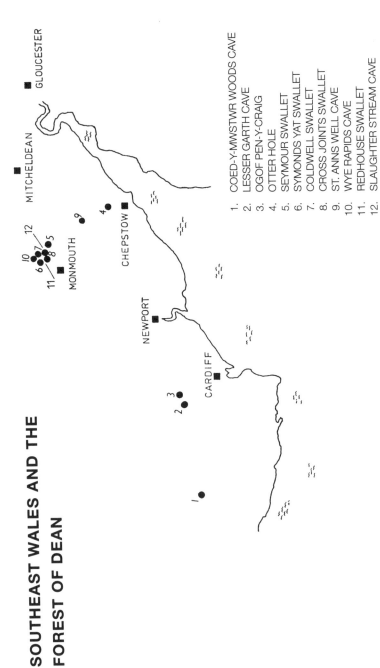

1. COED-Y-MWSTWR WOODS CAVE
2. LESSER GARTH CAVE
3. OGOF PEN-Y-CRAIG
4. OTTER HOLE
5. SEYMOUR SWALLET
6. SYMONDS YAT SWALLET
7. COLDWELL SWALLET
8. CROSS JOINTS SWALLET
9. ST. ANNS WELL CAVE
10. WYE RAPIDS CAVE
11. REDHOUSE SWALLET
12. SLAUGHTER STREAM CAVE

1. Southeast Wales and the Forest of Dean

Ban-yr-Gore Cave

Grade 5

Grid Ref ST5472 9742   OS Maps 1:50000 sheet 162,
1:25000 Wye Valley & Forest of Dean O/L

Altitude : 10 metres

Length : 620 metres
Vertical Range : 100 metres

Location   The entrance is situated in the Wye Valley about 1.5 kilometres upstream from Otter Hole.
Description   An extremely tight and tortuous cave which should be avoided in wet weather.
A 5m excavated drop leads to a small passage with a tight squeeze, The Stopper, after about 75m. Further thrutching along a very narrow rift then leads to a larger passage, First Respite. Beyond this the passage soon lowers again before regaining a high narrow rift and a climb up to Second Respite. Beyond Second Respite the rift narrows again and has been enlarged by banging. After a long struggle a chamber, named The Largest So Far and measuring 1m wide and 12m high, is entered. *A climb up near the start of the chamber leads to John's Rift which heads back towards the entrance for 90m.* At the end of The Largest So Far a 10m climb up leads to the Upper Rift. *A further climb leads to Paul's Passage, 36m of very tight inlet tube.*
A combination of traversing and walking on jammed boulders in the Upper Rift then leads to the Black Hole. By continuing straight ahead to the end of the rift a small tube, known as The Real Cave, goes off to the left and leads to a small active streamway. Upstream ends at a pool and downstream goes through a blasted calcite blockage to an inclined rift and then the Lower Rat Run which connects back to the Black Hole.
History   Discovered in 1982 by RFDCC after 7 years digging at the entrance. Survey by Paul Taylor

Coldwell Swallet

Grade 3/4

Grid Ref SO5690 1550   OS Maps 1:50000 sheet 162,
1:25000 Wye Valley & Forest of Dean O/L

Altitude : 114 metres

Length : 100 metres approx.
Vertical Range : 51 metres

Location   Situated near the cliff top path to the east of Symonds Yat. A small stream is followed down through undergrowth to where it sinks under a low arch.
Description   An immature cave which is regularly blocked with flood debris. The water has been tested to Slaughter Rising about 1.75 km distant in the Wye Valley.
A gently descending stooping size passage leads to a junction. Turn right into a low bedding plane for about 8 m and then bear left to a narrow slot. Drop down

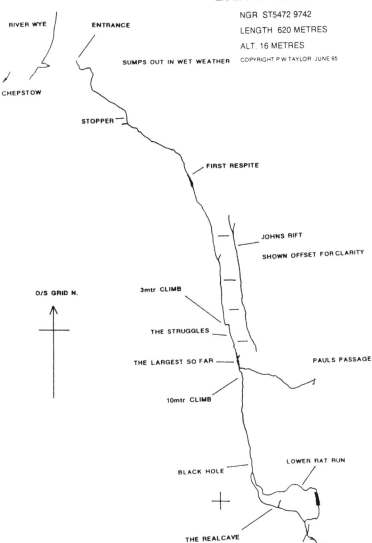

BAN-Y-GOR CAVE

NGR ST5472 9742

LENGTH 620 METRES

ALT. 16 METRES

COPYRIGHT P W TAYLOR JUNE 95

MONMOUTH

RIVER WYE

CHEPSTOW

ENTRANCE

SUMPS OUT IN WET WEATHER

STOPPER

FIRST RESPITE

JOHNS RIFT

SHOWN OFFSET FOR CLARITY

O/S GRID N.

3mtr CLIMB

THE STRUGGLES

THE LARGEST SO FAR

PAULS PASSAGE

10mtr CLIMB

BLACK HOLE

LOWER RAT RUN

THE REALCAVE

BASED ON AN ORIGINAL SURVEY AT 1:600.FROM CAVING SHOPS OR PAUL TAYLOR 01452 505673.

the slot to a 6 m free-climbable pitch where care is needed as you go into the pitch feet first. At the bottom, a rift up to 12 m high leads to a crawl turning right for about 6 m (this crawl sometimes silts up). A 2.5 m free-climbable pitch follows. Turn left for a short distance to a tight section of passage and then a small chamber. A crawl leads off from the chamber for about 3 m via a 90 degree bend, passable only by persons of small build. A very tight slot then drops immediately to the top of the final pitch which is 25 m deep (belay above the slot). At the bottom of the shaft the cave ends at a pool.

Tackle   Final Pitch – 25 m ladder, belay and lifeline.

History   Discovered by HCC. Extended by GSS.

Coed-y-Mwstwr Woods Cave   Grade 3
Alternative name : Pencoed Cave

Grid Ref SS9510 8090 OS Maps 1:50000 sheet 170, 1:25000 sheet SS/98	
Length : 180 metres approx.	

Location   The cave is situated in Coed-y-Mwstwr woods, marked on OS maps, which is near Pencoed. From the A473 Bridgend to Pencoed road, a track leads from just outside the village of Coychurch, over the railway, and into the woods. The entrance is situated in a small cliff within the woods and is on the right-hand side of the track.

Access   The cave lies on land belonging to Coed-y-Mwstwr Farm which is situated at SS947 809 to the west of the woods. Permission to visit the cave should be sought at the farm. The farmer has complained about damage to fences etc. and so care should be taken when crossing the land.

Description   The first part of the cave consists of a single passage about 50 m long which ends in a large chamber by a boulder collapse. *There is a short oxbow in the left-hand wall which contains some fine botryoidal stalactites which are also evident elsewhere in the lower parts of the cave.*

Above the boulder fall an 8 m crawl continues and gives access to the 18 m high Collapsed Rift. The crawl ends in boulders when it dips and turns back on itself. Just before a squeeze in the crawl, a hole on the right leads to a very unstable rift. Squeezing and scrambling over boulders gives access to the First Roof Chamber which is fairly large and close to the surface. At the near end of this chamber, a slot in the floor leads to another lower chamber.

To the left of the second chamber, an 18 m long tight descending rift passage leads to the continuation of the entrance passage beyond the boulder fall. This passage is stable, about 1.5 x 2.5 m, and leads after 22 m to a large chamber. Following this a 2.5 m drop over boulders leads to a narrower passage which terminates in a boulder choke chamber. Above this is a hole in the roof which leads to a series of small chambers connected by crawls. *Back at the start of the stable passage and to the left, leads to the large Middle Chamber which is 9 m wide, 18 m long, and 2.5 m high. It closes to a tight bedding plane containing some fine crystal pools.*

History   Survey by K.Jones and J.Mothersale.

WARNING :   The boulder fall area is extremely unstable.

Croes Bleddyn Swallet
Alternative name : Beaver Hole

Grade 3

Grid Ref ST4942 9620   OS Maps 1:50000 sheet 162,
1:25000 Wye Valley & Forest of Dean O/L

Altitude : 120 metres

Length : 151 metres

Location   Situated near Croes Bleddyn Farm to the north of the B4293 about 4 km from Chepstow. Take the track running north from the hamlet of Croes Bleddyn, opposite the turning to Itton, to a pair of gates. Between the gates is the entry to Llanquilan House. The sink is in the copse a few metres back along the track and can be seen from the track.
Access   The cave is gated and locked. Access on behalf of the landowner is via RFDCC.
Description   A 6 m easily climbable scaffolded shaft and a 4 m stooping tunnel lead to a short drop into a decorated breakdown chamber 10 m long and 3 m wide. There is evidence of roof collapse and the broken columns can be seen beneath the boulder floor. The stream appears from beneath boulders and the route continues to a decorated dry oxbow in a wide bedding plane streamway. After two bends, the roof lowers into the First Duck which is liable to sump and may require bailing. The stream then sinks preventing further progress.
Immediately after the First Duck, an abrupt left turn leads into the Second Duck (Mud Sump). This can be filled with evil-smelling liquid mud in a down and up crawling passageway leading into Scargill Passage. As the stream sinks, a hole to the left also accesses Scargill Passage which continues as a dry often low and stony passage under a boulder ruckle. Soon, a second stream enters from the left and the passage becomes more comfortable as the stream flows through a short series of little potholes and pools on its way to an impenetrable bedding with a static sump on the left. Immediately prior to this, a dry passage on the left, past formations, leads to a slot in the left wall which can be entered to access a lower level passage which leads to the Third Duck (Far Duck).
The Third Duck is a tight crawl over static water and leads to a straight 10 m passage ending in two dig sites.
History   The cave was first entered in 1979 as far as the First Duck. Extended in 1985. Survey to the First Duck 1980 (Geh & Shapter), survey beyond the First Duck in preparation.
WARNING : The cave is liable to flood in the middle section and is best accessed after the beginning of May.

Cross Joints Swallet

Grade 4

Grid Ref SO5622 1385   OS Maps 1:50000 sheet 162,
1:25000 Wye Valley & Forest of Dean O/L

Altitude : 106 metres

Length : 170 metres

Location   Situated in Mailscot Wood and is best approached by the track which runs from Hillersland to the Slaughter in the Wye Valley. A surface stream runs on the right of the track and the entrance to the cave is a sink in the left bank. A dam and diversion trench have been constructed around the entrance.

Description   The cave consists of a single passage which leads to a pitch into a large chamber. The water has been tested to Slaughter Rising in the Wye Valley. The first section of the cave is mostly flat out crawl with several tight squeezes. The stream is met entering from the left and the streamway then continues alternatively low and wide or high and narrow. After about 100 m, a boulder choke is passed through a tight squeeze. Beyond, the passage becomes a much larger walking size passage and is followed to the head of an 11 m pitch into a large, 15 m diameter chamber known as Hyperspace. The chamber marks the present end of the cave.

History   The cave was discovered by BUSS in 1972 and later extended by CPG and SUSS. Survey CPG/SUSS in 1977 & 1981.

Itton North Swallet   Grade 4

Grid Ref ST4903 9575   OS Maps 1:50000 sheet 162,
                                                     1:25000 Wye Valley & Forest of Dean O/L

Altitude : 109 metres

Length : 300 metres approx.

Location   The entrance is situated in the bottom of a wooded depression 500 m south of Itton Village Hall (on unclassified road from Chepstow to Devauden).

Access   The entrance is gated at the request of the landowner. For access details contact Hades Caving Club.

Description   An immature cave carrying a stream which has been traced to the inner end of Tunnels Left in Otter Hole.

An excavated 6 m entrance shaft with fixed ladder leads to a descent through boulders. After 8 m the stream enters through the roof. Downstream is an artificially widened rift for about 140 m, following the streambed for much of the way. This then develops into a tortuous narrow streamway which is followed for 100 m or so. The present end is a tight rift which is being spasmodically worked on to enlarge it.

History   Discovered in 1977 by Hades C.C.

WARNING : Care is needed – loose rocks.

Lesser Garth Cave   Grade 3/4
Alternative name : Ogof Tynant

Grid Ref ST1240 8230   OS Maps 1:50000 sheet 171, 1:25000 sheet ST/18

Length : 250 metres approx.

Location   Situated in Garth Wood which is marked on OS maps. At Morganstown, just off the A470 near Taff's Well, a footpath behind the Tynant Inn leads past allotments to the woods. Climb straight up the hill and the entrance is near the top in a shallow depression. Not easy to spot until you are right on top of it.

Description   An interesting and well decorated cave which lies very close to the active quarry and may be in danger of being destroyed.

The low entrance leads to a section of wide passage ending at a boulder platform overlooking the large Main Chamber. *To the left is a 9 m pitch into a narrow rift which runs back towards the entrance and also in the opposite direction. Going away from the entrance the passage can be followed via a tortuous rift with some squeezes to eventually emerge in a sizeable passage which was originally well decorated and formed on two levels. This is Ogof Ffynnon Taf, originally discovered via an entrance in the quarry which has now been destroyed and blocked by further quarrying. Sadly, many of the formations have also been ruined by vandals. To the left, the passage can be followed for about 60 m and ends in a boulder choke. To the right, a tight squeeze leads into a boulder chamber, this area being very unstable due to blasting.*

From the boulder platform, an old steel cable can be used to aid descent to the floor of the Main Chamber, however if an aid is required it is probably safer to fix your own rope. The Main Chamber is about 12 m high and 4 to 5 m wide with flowstone and curtains running down the walls. In one direction a narrow rift runs back towards the surface but continuing along the chamber, climbing up and down over boulders, leads to a bend where the passage becomes narrower. *To the right is a narrow oxbow passage which rejoins the main passage at a small chamber further on.* Straight ahead the main passage continues as a lofty rift and leads to a climb down to a stal floor. There are some fine formations high in the roof including an excellent calcite pillar above a huge wedged boulder. Just beyond this a small chamber is entered and the oxbow joins on the right. *A climb up through boulders leads to a bedding plane which soon becomes blocked.* The main passage continues at floor level but is now much smaller and soon ends at a large boulder choke.

Tackle   Rift Pitch – 10 m ladder or rope, belay and lifeline

History   The main cave has been known for a long time. Ogof Ffynnon Taf explored by Isca C.C. in 1986. Survey – Main cave by Dyffryn High S.S. in 1968. Ogof Ffynnon Taf by Isca C.C. in 1986.

Ogof Pen-Y-Craig   Grade 2

Grid Ref ST1270 8220   OS Maps 1:50000 sheet 171, 1:25000 sheet ST/18

Length : 90 metres approx.

Location   Situated in an old quarry to the west of and near to Lesser Garth Cave. The entrance is at the northern end of the quarry and near to the top. Access is gained by crossing a loose scree slope a long way above the quarry floor to the rock face in which there are several small holes. The entrance is a low slot and involves a short but tricky climb.

Description   A small but very well decorated cave which is protected to a certain extent by its location. Probably associated with the nearby Lesser Garth Cave but there is no known connection.

A squeeze through the entrance leads to a small passage. An easy squeeze to the left then leads through boulders to the large main passage. Two routes lead on in the lofty rift passage, an obvious lower one below the boulders and a less obvious one above the boulders. Both meet up and the passage becomes lower. Straight ahead a shattered rock window gives access to a small grotto while slightly to the right a low wide bedding plane crawl leads to a small chamber. At

the far side of the chamber an awkward squeeze down through boulders leads to a finely decorated grotto with some long straws and a profusion of white stals.
History   Discovered by a member of SWCC in 1977.

Otter Hole   Grade 5

Grid Ref ST5258 9615   OS Maps 1:50000 sheet 162,
                                     1:25000 Wye Valley & Forest of Dean O/L

Altitude : 18 metres

Length : 3352 metres

Location   The entrance is situated in the bank of the River Wye near St.Arvans. From Chepstow, take the A466 towards St.Arvans and then Tintern. About 1.6 km outside St.Arvans, at the top of a wooded hill, is a forestry commission car park at Wyndcliff on the right. A track leads from the car park, down through the trees, towards the Wye. Go past a pump house and then over a log bridge. Just beyond the bridge a rough track on the left descends steeply to the river. Follow the track along the river bank to a small cliff. The entrance to the cave is at the foot of the cliff.
Access   The cave is gated and access controlled to preserve the cave and its decorations. Contact John Hutchinson, 4 Redwood Close, Chepstow, Gwent NP6 5RJ, stating a choice of preferred dates and enclosing an SAE. A guide will be provided and ample notice should be given so that the necessary arrangements can be made.
The first sump (Tidal Sump) is affected by the level of the River Wye outside. The sump closes approx. 3 hours before high tide and opens again 3 hours after high tide. It is not normally free-diveable. The times of the tides can be found in Arrowsmith's Tide Tables for the Bristol and Channel Ports. If these are not available, ask for tidal information when writing for access. The cave should not be entered on high tides of more than 14.9 metres as the entrance series floods.
Description   The cave is one of the most serious undertakings in the country, mainly due to the complications of the tidal sump, and should only be attempted by experienced cavers. There are also several instances of cavers being ill after a trip in the cave, the source of the illness being as yet unknown. However, the cave is probably the most beautifully decorated cave in the UK, and well worth braving the hazards.
The walk-in entrance leads quickly to a climb up into a bedding plane on the left. At the end of this is a climb down into a lower, extremely muddy, bedding plane. The bedding plane contains pools and a large plastic pipe which is used for rescue purposes. The way on is to follow the pipe – it is only necessary to leave the pipe in two places, at a tight squeeze and at a climb over a boulder. The bedding plane emerges into a small chamber and the way on is via a rift on the right known as Fossil Passage. It is worth memorising this section for the return journey as the way back is not obvious. Fossil Passage is followed via a very slippery 2.4 m climb and a step over a hole to a long section of muddy walking and crawling past mud stained formations to the Tidal Sump. This can be passed as the tide is going down by swimming across to an eye hole or you can wait for half an hour or so and walk through the bottom.
Beyond the sump, a climb up a mud bank on the right and down into a muddy

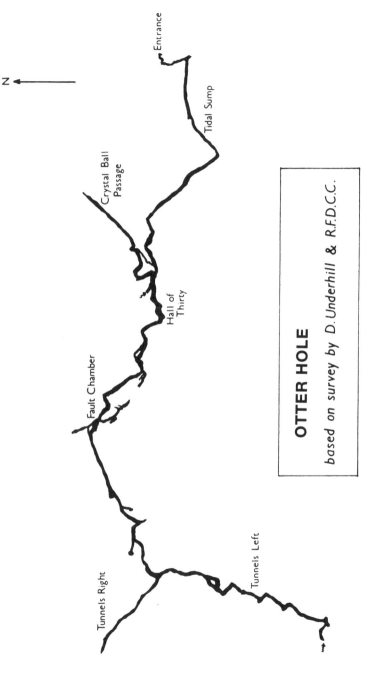

OTTER HOLE

based on survey by D.Underhill & R.F.D.C.C.

passage leads to an iron ladder. Climb up the ladder and continue in an upstream direction (behind you as you come up the ladder). After about 10 m a climb up through boulders on the left leads to a small chamber where there is a food dump (this is intended for real emergency use and not for parties who have just missed the tide). On the other side of the chamber is a squeeze followed by a drop. Traverse around this on the left and climb down through boulders to the stream. A short section of stream passage is then followed to a boulder pile. Climb this and then traverse above the stream to a boulder floored chamber, beyond which is a pleasant section of streamway. Towards the end, a climb up through boulders on the right leads to a bedding chamber marked by a cairn. Turn left into another chamber, on the other side of which is Choke 2. The choke is unstable and care must be taken. A route through the choke leads to a squeeze up into a chamber with a boulder slope. At the top of the boulders a fixed electron ladder leads back to the stream. *Straight ahead leads to Sump 2 which is 0.6 m long and free diveable. After a further 18 m Sump 3 is met.* **SUMP 3 AND BEYOND IS ONLY ACCESSIBLE TO DIVERS. THIS IS 12 M LONG TO A LARGE AIRBELL IMMEDIATELY FOLLOWED BY SUMP 4 WHICH IS 6 M LONG WITH AN AWKWARD SQUEEZE. THE STREAMWAY IS THEN FOLLOWED FOR 165 M TO SUMP 5 WHICH IS 35 M LONG WHICH HAS BEEN DIVED TO A SMALL AIRBELL WITH A LARGE MUD BANK IN FRONT OF A SMALL INLET WHICH HAS NOT BEEN DIVED. BEYOND THE AIRBELL IS SUMP 6, 40 M LONG, LEADING TO A CANAL. AFTER 55 M AN AWKWARD DUCK IS NEGOTIATED TO REACH SUMP 7 WHICH IS AN ONGOING DIVE CURRENTLY ABOUT 130 M FROM BASE.** Almost immediately after the ladder pitch into the stream a rift passage at eye level on the right leads up to The Extension. Follow the rift upwards to the bottom of a boulder choke. A tortuous climb up through the choke leads to a small rift. Immediately behind ones head is a tricky climb up over a stal encrusted boulder into an L-shaped chamber. Turning left into the bottom of the L, a climb up boulders leads to a hole going down behind a boulder. Drop through the hole and cross a small chamber then climb back up again to the start of a crawl. Follow this to a tight squeeze and an easier passage. Almost immediately on the left are several holes leading to a bedding chamber. Take the easiest one. The bedding chamber is the start of the Extension and from here the cave changes character completely. *On the right, a tube leads via a climb and a squeeze down through very loose boulders to Crystal Balls Passage with its fine pom-pom formations.* Straight across the bedding chamber, a taped path leads past increasingly magnificent formations to a large boulder floored chamber with enormous curtains in the roof. Crossing the chamber on the left leads to the Hall of Thirty with its large and magnificent stalagmite bosses. Follow the path on the left-hand side to the top of the chamber which provides a fantastic view. A hole then leads via some crawling amidst formations to The Camp. Here there is an emergency food dump and the sound of dripping water. Follow the sound of the water, up a boulder slope, to a collection of mugs and containers collecting the drips. The water, which is scarce in this part of the cave, appears to be safe to drink.

Crossing the chamber containing the mugs leads to a short section of sandy crawling on the right followed by more walking size passage for some distance to Fault Chamber. This is a large collapse chamber marked by a cairn. There are some short side passages on the left and right but by crossing the chamber one reaches another section of decorations starting with some gours. A climb down into a rift past much stal and an immediate re-ascent over a steep stal flow leads to Long Straw Chamber. This chamber is entered by stepping over a pool surrounded by stal, and care must be taken. The left wall and most of the floor of the chamber is covered by flowstone with numerous 5 m long straws hanging from the roof. Follow the taped path along the right-hand wall to a descent behind a huge block into a well decorated rift. The passage becomes blocked by flowstone. Do not climb over this but go through a hole low down on the left into a rift and then a short rope climb leads back into the passage. There is a choked rift on the right but the main passage continues with more formations to a chamber containing a large pool with two fine red rimstone fans. The passage continues to a major junction and another change in character.

The impressive boulder floored passage straight ahead is Tunnels Left. This leads for some distance through mainly large passage with short sections of crawl to the end of the cave and a short streamway. Downstream, the water disappears into a large boulder choke. **UPSTREAM, A SUMP HAS BEEN PASSED BY DIVERS FOR 15 M TO A LARGE AIRBELL. A SECOND SUMP FOLLOWS WHICH IS 33 M LONG AND 12 M DEEP TO A LARGE AVEN. THIS IS FOLLOWED BY A THIRD SUMP WHICH HAS BEEN DIVED FOR 53 M.**

Back at the junction, the passage on the right is Tunnels Right and leads through crawls to a well decorated rift and eventually to the Crystal Bath. This is a large crystal pool and can be passed with great care on the right. The passage beyond ends at a static sump.

History   The cave was first discovered by GSS and RFDCC in 1970. Extensive digging by RFDCC led to major extensions in 1974 and 1975. Survey by RFDCC in 1978.

Redhouse Lane Swallet

Grade 4

Grid Ref SO5734 1499   OS Maps 1:50000 sheet 162,
1:25000 Wye Valley & Forest of Dean O/L

Altitude : 95 metres

Length : 1615 metres
Vertical Range : 40 metres

Location   Turn left into Redhouse Lane from the road heading north through English Bicknor and take the next right turn, a single track lane. Proceed past Bicknor Farm to park by the next gateway on the left. Go through the gate and walk alongside the fence towards an obvious large wooded depression where the entrance is situated.

Access   The cave is locked and ís an active dig by the RFDCC. Access is on an appointed leader basis and is controlled by Paul Taylor, 9 Massey Road, Gloucester GL1 4LG. Six weeks notice is required. Wetsuits are advisable from the Main Stream Inlet above The Junction. No novices are allowed beyond the end of the Marden Streamway. From here wetsuits are essential. The cave is liable to be closed for lengthy periods during the winter months owing to high water levels.

Description   The cave carries a stream which has been tested to the Slaughter Rising in the Wye Valley.

The Entrance Shaft descends 10 m via a concrete tube with stirrups, followed by a fixed ladder to the First Landing. From this artificial landing two routes descend to the Mud Duck.

REDHOUSE LANE SWALLET

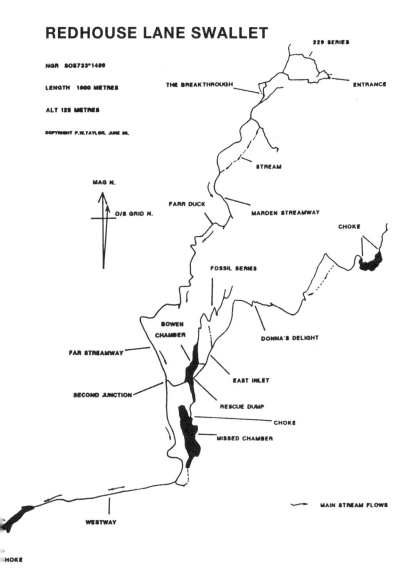

NGR SO5733*1489

LENGTH 1000 METRES

ALT 125 METRES

COPYRIGHT P.W.TAYLOR, JUNE 96.

229 SERIES

THE BREAKTHROUGH

ENTRANCE

STREAM

MAG N.

O/S GRID N.

FARR DUCK

MARDEN STREAMWAY

CHOKE

FOSSIL SERIES

BOWEN CHAMBER

FAR STREAMWAY

DONNA'S DELIGHT

EAST INLET

SECOND JUNCTION

RESCUE DUMP

CHOKE

MISSED CHAMBER

WESTWAY

MAIN STREAM FLOWS

CHOKE

BASED ON AN ORIGINAL SURVEY AT 1:1000.FROM CAVING SHOPS OR PAUL TAYLOR 01452 505673.

THE OLD ROUTE

From the first landing, a 2 m fixed ladder descends to the Second Landing. A climb down via scaffolding then leads to the top of a short series of squeezes descending under shored-up boulders which lie in Horror Chamber. From the bottom the cave levels out as a crawl leads into the 3 m high First Chamber. *A short passage leads off to the right to access an aven,* whereas the main route is a 3.5 m descent at the far end of the chamber to a flat-out crawl ending in Fair Chamber. *From here a passage on the right again leads to an aven.*

From Fair Chamber, a low crawl marks the start of The Mud Canal which is dry as long as the surface water remains diverted. After 20 m the passage bends into a continuing crawl where the New Route enters after a few metres from the right.

THE NEW ROUTE

The 2m high Entrance Rift leads off from the First Landing through a series of three right-angled bends leading into Anniversary Rift. At the point of entry into this rift a 3m chimney leads downwards into the Christmas Extension, commencing with the 3m deep Tango Rift and a climb down past loose boulders into a small chamber. *Routes to the left lead into a tight network of interconnecting crawls.*

Low down on the right in the chamber an excavated crawl leads into 229 Series where Rope Pitch, a 3m fixed rope descent, enters a larger chamber. A climb down over the boulders at the far end leads into a flat-out crawl which ends in a brief ascent to a stalagmite barrier. *The passage to the right, a decorated inlet, leads to a bedding choked in wet mud.* By continuing ahead at the stalagmite barrier a low passage leads down to the crawl at the end of the Mud Canal.

DOUBLE ANNIVERSARY SERIES AND MARDEN STREAMWAY

From the junction of the two routes of entry, a stooping passage containing a small stream, lowers to eventually reach a constriction. Before this constriction, just following a flat-out crawl, The Mud Duck, an ascent up a slope on the left leads to the Upper Dry Crawl which regains the stream beyond the constriction. From here a low bedding crawl over shingle leads into the Main Stream Inlet *which can be followed for 12m and arrives from the left.* A wet crawl leads on to The Junction where the route continues, dry, to the right. *The Main Stream flows ahead at the Junction to sink under the right-hand wall. The passage however continues as an inlet and can be followed upstream through a duck, which can be awkward in high water conditions, to a final upstream sump pool.*

By turning right at the Junction, a dry hands and knees crawl leads after 15 m to a lower crawl over sand to an oxbowed section. The passage continues to a wet section and the main stream is found once again at the Marden Streamway, a wide but low passage progressing into a more comfortable section of streamway. *A climb in the roof of the passage leads into a boulder ruckle.* The streamway continues into deeper water through a right-angled bend before finishing in the Farr Duck (8m long) which has a limited airspace in high water conditions (fixed guideline).

FAR STREAMWAY AND WESTWAY

Beyond Farr Duck lies a series of bends in a low streamway for 100 m over beds of gravel and mud, interspersed by a series of further ducks, some with limited airspace. From Sponge Corner the passage becomes walking size as a 30 m rift leads towards the Second Junction where a passage leads off to the left into the Fossil Series.

The streamway continues from the Second Junction for a further 110 m to an area of breakdown with a short dry passage entering from the left. Westway continues to the right, 3 m high and 4 m wide, past further areas of breakdown for about 170 m. The stream takes a lower course in the passage passing from one side to the other and eventually taking a course low on the right which can be accessed at various points. The passage continues past a mud bank with cooling tower mud formations just before an abrupt halt at a boulder choke which has been penetrated to a continuation which is currently being dug.

At the choke, a drop down into a narrow rift on the right regains the stream which follows into a thin rift with black walls ending after a further 60 m in a deep water duck.

FOSSIL SERIES

From the Second Junction a crawl and a short passage lead to the 10m wide and 8m high Bowen Chamber with a large bank of dried mud in dominance on the left. *By climbing the slope opposite the mud bank a crawl leads to the bottom of a dangerous boulder choke where a carefully picked route upwards emerges into Missed Chamber, 50m long, 10m wide and 6m high, ending in breakdown.* By continuing ahead from Bowen Chamber a small inlet stream, East Inlet, may be accessed, but this is better done by climbing up the mud bank and turning right at the first opportunity.

By climbing up the mud bank and keeping to the right to preserve the mud floor, a sizeable dry fossil passage can be followed for 100m to a complex series of passages in an area of breakdown. By following the more obvious route to the right a tight section leads down into the East Inlet.

EAST INLET

This small streamway consists of an uncomfortable grovel in a low stream over gravel beds and around boulders for 60m to reach a long canal section, Donna's Delight, which easily becomes a duck after prolonged or heavy rain. As this section is in excess of 50m long it should be treated with respect! Twisting and turning sharply, the section is a hands and knees crawl leading to a low wet creep which opens up into the side of Surprise Passage.

To the left a rift leads to a crawl and a dig site, whereas the tunnel-like passage leads on to the right to a sharp bend into a stooping stream passage ending in a consolidated boulder fall. By ascending the slope on the left a dry bypass leads from initial crawling into a comfortable dry passage to a sandy tunnel, 5 Hour Dig, which regains the stream.

Continuing up this inlet leads through a boulder choke to a wide flat-roofed chamber. At the far end of the chamber a route through a shorter choke leads to a final boulder fall. Both these chokes are extremely dangerous!

History   After numerous attempts over a protracted period to open up the swallet, a determined project was commenced by RFDCC in 1990. The Christmas Extension was first entered in late 1991. The passages beyond the Mud Canal were entered in 1992 and East Inlet in 1993. Survey by Paul Taylor.

WARNING : The cave contains a number of ducks which are liable to flooding and should only be entered in dry and settled weather. If the surface diversion pipes are removed the main stream will enter the cave at an earlier stage and the cave is liable to flood in both routes in the early sections. There is an emergency dump in Bowen Chamber.

Seymour Swallet   Grade 3

Grid Ref SO5910 1390   OS Maps 1:50000 sheet 162,
                                   1:25000 Wye Valley & Forest of Dean O/L

Altitude : 152 metres

Length : 106 metres approx.
Vertical Range : 54 metres

Location   Situated near Edge End on the A4136 Monmouth to Mitcheldean road. A narrow track leads from the main road to Hoarthorn's Farm and the cave is situated at the end of a valley below Hoarthorn's Wood behind the farm. The entrance is on the left-hand side of the valley and is covered by a lid set in concrete.
Access   Ask for permission at Hoarthorn's Farm.
Description   An interesting system of rift passages which takes large quantities of water during floods.
An easy entrance shaft leads to a continuing and obvious descent through boulders to the top of a large rift chamber. A climb down a fixed ladder leads to a ledge and the way on is to the right along a narrow crawl. The crawl leads to a junction where the obvious way on to the right soon ends at a small chamber. A less obvious way over boulders to the left leads to a descent in a narrow rift. The rift is followed to a low arch on the left which leads to a muddy passage and a high rift which marks the end of the cave. The rift can be climbed to the right but to the left it closes down within a few metres. *There are several side passages off the main route but all become blocked or too tight.*
History   The cave was first explored by GSS. Dug spasmodically by several clubs but main extensions made by GSS.

Slaughter Stream Cave   Grade 3
Alternative name : Wet Sink

Grid Ref SO5820 1375   OS Maps 1:50000 sheet 162,
                                   1:25000 Wye Valley & Forest of Dean O/L

Length : 11,000 metres +
Vertical Range : 100 metres

Location   The entrance is situated in a copse at the bottom of a field to the east of the Joyford to English Bicknor lane in the Forest of Dean. From the field gateway follow the footpath down the side of the field and then cross to a stile on the right. The entrance (Wet Sink) is a large shaft some 100 m to the left of the stile.
Access   The cave is gated and access is controlled on behalf of the landowner by RFDCC. For details contact Andy Clark, Sunshade Cottage, Lower Redbrook, Monmouth, Gwent NP5 4LZ enclosing an S.A.E.
Description   The 20 m deep entrance shaft is descended by a series of fixed ladders to reach a gate at the bottom. A squeeze through a small rift then leads

to the top of a 10 m pitch, again with a fixed ladder, into Mouse Aven. Directly under the pitch is an excavated passage through a choke. Care is needed here and in the next part of the cave as there is a large amount of loose material. A climb down on the right then leads to a short pitch where a 3 m ladder and spreader are required. This leads to Balcony Chamber at the top of a 12 m pitch to the base of another aven. Belay to fixed hangers on both pitches. At the bottom of the aven, a climb down leads to a small stream which is followed through a crawl to the main Slaughter Stream at Cross Stream Junction.

DOWNSTREAM SERIES

Downstream, a large walking size passage is followed until the water gets deeper just before the Cascade, a waterfall issuing from the roof which is best passed on the right. Continuing beyond the Cascade, a junction is reached with another stream entering from the left. *This is East Stream Passage which can be followed for 300 m until it ends at the base of two large avens.*

Continuing down the main stream the water gets deep in a few places before disappearing into Sump 1. **SUMP 1 HAS NOT BEEN DIVED.** About 100 m before Sump 1, a crawl leads off to the right over sand, to enter the Dryslade Series which bypasses the sump. The crawl soon increases in size and a walking passage continues to a dry, fossil sump. Passing this on the right, a junction is reached with Coal Seam Passage. *This can be followed to the right for 400 m to a choke which can be passed via an excavated hole to link with a passage off The Chunnel in the Upstream Series.* 100 m after this junction, *a 2 m climb on the left leads to a sandy crawl and a very loose 10 m climb up into Pirate Passage. This can be followed for some considerable distance and ends about 200 m away from the Seymour/Hawthorns Wood area.* The main route continues through increasingly large passage before eventually rejoining the main streamway just beyond Sump 2. **SUMP 2 IS 4 M LONG IN A LOW PASSAGE AND SURFACES IN A CANAL. THE CONTINUING PASSAGE, CALLED DRAKES SERIES, CONTINUES UPSTREAM VIA SOME CHAMBERS FOR ABOUT 300 M TO A DEEP POOL WHERE WATER WELLS UP. THIS HAS NOT BEEN DIVED BUT WILL ALMOST CERTAINLY LEAD TO SUMP 1. HOWEVER, MORE WATER COMES OUT THAN GOES IN AT SUMP 1 AND SO THERE MAY BE OTHER INLETS ON THE WAY.**

Continuing down the main stream, the passage reaches heights of up to 15 m and there are a number of strangely shaped rock sculptures in a part of the passage known as the Sculpture Trail. At an obvious right-angled bend just beyond two deep pools, Echo Passage goes off to the left. *This can be followed to a choked sump and a dry upper series of passages which leads to a window overlooking the main stream.* Further down the main stream the roof starts to lower before eventually the water disappears into Sump 3. **SUMP 3 IS 11 M LONG FOLLOWED BY 20 M OF CANAL WITH ONLY SMALL AIRSPACE TO SUMP 4 WHICH IS VERY TIGHT AND 4 M LONG TO A SMALL AIRSPACE. SUMP 5 FOLLOWS IMMEDIATELY AND IS 18 M LONG INTO 30 M OF VERY LOW PASSAGE ENDING AT A VERY NARROW RIFT.** Just before reaching Sump 3, a sandy crawl on the right leads to a larger passage and continues down a series of drops to Kuwait Passage, which has jet black walls and helictite formations. After some considerable distance, a climb down leads to a rift and then a chamber. From here the character of the cave changes again, going through a series of tight rifts to meet a small canal which decreases in size until the roof meets the water at Static Sump 4. The passage prior to the sump is extremely muddy and at times the water obviously backs up over some considerable distance.

STATIC SUMP 4 HAS BEEN DIVED FOR ONLY A FEW METRES. THE SUMP IS ENTERED

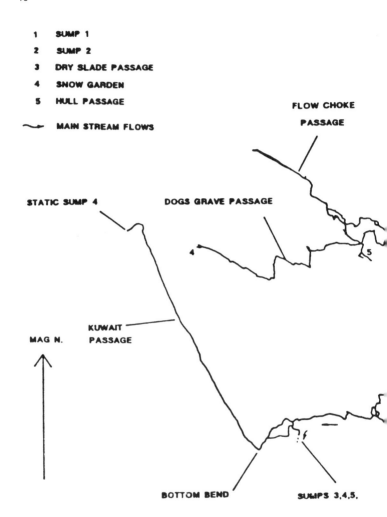

1   SUMP 1
2   SUMP 2
3   DRY SLADE PASSAGE
4   SNOW GARDEN
5   HULL PASSAGE

~→ MAIN STREAM FLOWS

FLOW CHOKE
PASSAGE

STATIC SUMP 4   DOGS GRAVE PASSAGE

4   5

MAG N.   KUWAIT
            PASSAGE

BOTTOM BEND   SUMPS 3,4,5.

BASED ON ORIGINAL SURVEY AT 1:1000.FROM CAVING SHOPS OR

PAUL TAYLOR 01452 50567

NGR SO5815 1372

LENGTH 12,000
METRES

ALT. 130 METRES

COPYRIGHT P.W.TAYLOR. JUNE 95

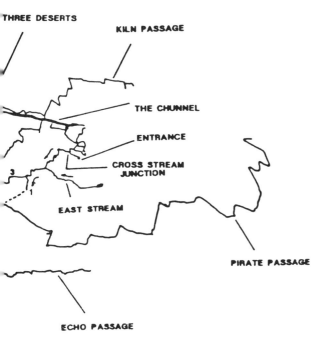

THREE DESERTS

KILN PASSAGE

THE CHUNNEL

ENTRANCE

CROSS STREAM
JUNCTION

EAST STREAM

PIRATE PASSAGE

ECHO PASSAGE

SLAUGHTER STREAM CAVE

THROUGH THE RIGHT WALL BUT THE WAY ON BECOMES BLOCKED BY LARGE MUD BANKS. This marks the present downstream end of the cave.

UPSTREAM SERIES

Upstream for Cross Stream Junction, a well decorated passage is followed to an obvious passage on the left. *This can be followed to an inlet through a loose boulder choke where extreme caution is needed. This leads to a small section of streamway ending in a sump. To the right of the choke a narrow crawl leads into a large, high chamber, with calcite formations in the roof.*

Continuing up the main stream, the passage becomes smaller and leads to a mud sump on the left. To the right, a crawl through water leads to the foot of Zurree Aven, an impressive 20 m high chamber with a stream cascading down the back wall. A climb up a series of waterfalls then gives access to the upper series of the cave.

At a point where the stream can be seen flowing down from the right, a dry climb up on the left (care needed at the top because of loose rocks) leads to a section of fossil streamway. The way on is a crawl through a choke on the right, leading to larger passages known as The Graveyard. *A rift to the left leads to a 10 m pitch and connection to the lower streamway.* A taped path leads through The Graveyard, past some bone deposits and a collection of stalagmites called the Gnome Garden, and continues to a junction with a larger passage called The Chunnel. The way on is to the left and the passage increases in size until it reaches 10 m wide and 5 m high. After some distance an obvious passage on the right is Kiln Passage. *This can be followed for 500 m via a mixture of walking size passage and sandy crawls to some traverses leading to a small streamway which eventually closes down.* Beyond the entrance to Kiln Passage, the Chunnel continues via a series of boulder slopes to end in an area of tight rifts and chokes. *Part way along, a passage on the left links with Coal Seam Passage in the Downstream Series.* About 70 m beyond the junction with Kiln Passage, a sandy crawl on the right-hand side of the Chunnel leads to the Three Deserts, three low sandy areas separated by piles of breakdown. Eventually, walking size passage is regained and is followed to a climb up a pile of loose rocks. The passage then forks with the way on being to the left. This is followed to an area of breakdown. *To the right leads to Flow Choke Extension, around 700 m of large passage and chambers ending at a choke completely sealed by flowstone.* To the left, the passage continues past the walled-in skeleton of a dog to a 2 m climb down under a large choke. At the bottom, a fossil stream passage continues and is intermittently blocked by large boulder piles, all of which can be passed. After about 150 m the passage ends at a narrow rift but a way on to the left leads into a high rift passage with large crystals growing from the walls. The passage continues to a sharp right-hand bend where a stream can be heard flowing at the bottom of a narrow rift. This rift has been enlarged and access to the stream can be made via a tight 10 m pitch. The main passage continues to reach a narrow rift decorated with helictites and a crystal floor known as The Snow Gardens which has been taped off to preserve the formations. This marks the present upstream end of the cave.

Tackle   Pitch below choke – 3 m ladder, belay and lifeline
Balcony Chamber Pitch – 12 m ladder, belay and lifeline

History   The entrance, known as Wet Sink, has been dug spasmodically by various clubs since the 1950's. The breakthrough into the cave was made by the JAGA group from the RFDCC in 1990. Survey by Paul Taylor 1995 available from caving shops.

St.Anns Well Cave

Grade 3

Grid Ref SO5798 0277   OS Maps 1:50000 sheet 162,
1:25000 Wye Valley & Forest of Dean O/L

Altitude : 150 metres

Length : 122 metres

Location   Situated on the edge of Pickethill Wood to the southwest of St.Briavels in the Forest of Dean. Take the road from St.Briavels towards Bream and after about 1.5 km turn right opposite Hoggins Farm. After about another 2.5 km take the first turning right onto a small side road leading to the wood.
Description   The cave is a resurgence in the Lower Limestone Shales and is low, wet and unstable.
A series of crawls and narrow rifts lead to a larger passage which terminates in a boulder collapse. The way on is not clear.

Symonds Yat Swallet

Grade 3

Grid Ref SO5630 1540   OS Maps 1:50000 sheet 162,
1:25000 Wye Valley & Forest of Dean O/L

Altitude : 91 metres

Length : 106 metres approx.

Location   From the main car park at Symonds Yat, follow the large forest trail to the south until it crosses a small stream. Follow the stream to the right until it sinks. The entrance to the cave is just beyond.
Description   This is a cave which contains many loose boulders and although some stabilising work has been carried out great care must be taken.
The entrance shaft drops down through boulders for about 9 m. At the bottom, a series of crawls with loose boulders leads to a large chamber called The Slaughterhouse.
History   First explored by BUSS.

Wye Rapids Cave (C3)

Grade 3

Grid Ref SO5610 1560   OS Maps 1:50000 sheet 162,
1:25000 Wye Valley & Forest of Dean O/L

Length : 91 metres

Location   Situated at Symonds Yat. There are a number of small caves and mines situated in the cliffs on the eastern bank of the River Wye near the old station. Some of the caves are numbered and Wye Rapids Cave bears the number C3.
Description   Just inside the entrance is a large chamber about 10 m square. On the far side of the chamber a narrow crawl which is tight in places is followed for about 25 metres to a complex of collapsed bedding planes and passages plus a chamber.

There is a voice connection with the neighbouring C2 cave.
History   Survey B.Whiting & R.Gillespie in 1979.

Lesser Caves and Sites of Speleological Interest

Bearse Pot   SO5730 0580
Blackcliff Cave   SO5336 9838
Bowyers Hole   SO5670 1600
Brockwells Quarry Cave   ST4750 8950
Candleston Castle Resurgence No.1   SS8705 7766
Candleston Castle Resurgence No.2   SS8712 7725
Castell Meredydd Resurgence   ST2267 8883
Cas Troggy   ST4592 9271
Coldwell Rocks Caves   SO567 157 to SO576 160
Corntown Resurgence   SS9200 7735
Crick Spring   ST4972 9118
Cursits Cave   SO6530 1110
Darkhill Cave   SO5676 0549
Diggers Hole   SO5470 1470
Dinham Sink   ST4742 9197
Dropping Wells   SO5530 1450
Dunraven Sea Caves   SS875 739
Font y Gary Caves   ST0502 6583
Frog Pot   SO5730 0580
Gelli Quarry Cave   ST1446 8327
Giant's Cave   ST5255 9628
Great Doward Cave   SO5440 1490
Green Moss Cave   SO5550 1410
Grey Hill Sinks   ST4322 9257
Highgrove Pothole   SO5720 0340
Hoarthorn's Wood Swallet   SO5910 1350
Itton South Sink   ST4907 9565
Kiln Hole   SO5840 1395
King Arthurs Cave   SO5450 1580
Little Gronda   ST4906 9357
Littel Hoggin Farm Pot   SO5730 0500
Llanfair Discoed Sinks   ST4408 9237
Llanquilan Quarry Sink   ST4949 9633
Merlins Cave   SO5560 1530
Merthyr Mawr Caves   SS887 769
Merthyr Mawr Village Resurgence   SS8865 7764
Milkwall Quarry Caves   SO5830 0890
Mounton Brook Sink   ST4951 9420
Mounton Brook Lower Sink   ST4997 9387
Mounton Brook Digs   ST4951 9420 & ST4967 9405
Nash Point Caves   SS9159 6821
Nedern Brook Sink   ST4860 8880
Newton Spring   SS8900 7700
Ogof Blaen Gwynlais   ST1440 8390

Ogof Castell y Dryn   ST0370 7240
Ogof Rhedyin   SO2741 0400
Ogof Santes Ddwynwen   SS9467 6769
Ogof Tynant Fechan   ST1250 8230
Ogof y Pant   SS7230 9780
Ogof yr Allt   SS7170 9750
Old Stone Well   SO5550 1275
Park Barn Sink   SO5638 0372
Patches Wood Caves   SO5500 1380
Penhow Sink   ST4204 9083
Red Hand Cave   ST1187 6616
Rhoose Caves   ST0631 6558
Rogerstone Grange Main Sink   ST5064 9665
Rogerstone Grange East Sink   ST5086 9653
Schwyll Risings   SS8873 7711
Seven Sisters Rock Shelters   SO546 158
Ship Rock Cave   SO5710 1560
Shorn Cliff Cave   ST5420 9910
Slade Brook Risings   SO5676 0553
Slade Wood Risings   SO5686 0535
Slaughter Rising   SO5554 1453
Sopers Pot   SO5580 1408
St.Arvans Main Sink   ST5138 9682
St.Arvans Lower Sink   ST5106 9646
St.Brides Mill Spring   ST4257 9013
St.Peters Cave   ST5389 9275
Stout Point cave   SS9724 6689
Symonds Yat Caves   SO5600 1400
Three J's Grotto   SO5590 1530
Tintern Quarry Caves   ST5470 9780
Tredegar Wood North Sink   ST4917 9292
Tredegar Wood South Sink   ST4904 9265
Upper Rodge Wood Cave   ST4670 8970
Wellhead Resurgence   ST5013 9420
Whippington Brook Rising   SO5532 1408
Whippington Brook Swallet   SO5510 1370
Whirley Holes Resurgence   ST4700 9000
Whitebrook Sink   ST4219 9218
Willscroft Wood Pots   SO5680 0480
Wyastone Whitebeam Cave   SO5420 1560
Wyndcliff Cave   ST5279 9744
Wyndcliff Quarry Caves   ST5280 9735

2. Clydach Gorge Area

Cwmavon Quarry Cave

Grade 2

Alternative name: Ogof Cwmavon

Grid Ref SO2720 0740   OS Maps 1:50 000 sheet 161, 1:25 000 sheet SO/20

Altitude: 336 metres

Length: 91 metres approx.

Location   This cave is situated several kilometres to the south-east of the gorge, in Cwm Afon about 2.5 km from Blaenavon. An old quarry incline starts from the A4043 near Cwmavon reservoir. Follow the incline to a forestry track then turn left. After about 100 metres, a track goes up on the right by the remains of some old buildings. Follow the track to a clearing then head straight up the hill to an old quarry. The entrances to the cave are situated in this quarry face.

Description   The cave is totally dry throughout and is a good cave for beginners. There are three entrances to the cave. The left hand entrance leads via a narrow rift passage to a pot. It is possible to traverse over the pot and climb down from the other side to a rubble heap at the bottom. Continuing on from the other side of the pot is a narrow passage which passes another entrance on the right. A little further on, another passage from the third entrance comes in from the right. The way on becomes a crawl for a short distance and leads to a high rift passage which gradually peters out. Near the end, a passage on the right leads to a narrow rift which can be descended by traversing along the top and climbing down on the far side. At the bottom the rift ends in boulders.

Elm Hole

Grade 3

Grid Ref SO2150 1246   OS Maps 1:50 000 sheet 161,
1:25 000 Brecon Beacons Eastern O/L

Altitude: 209 metres

Length: 680 metres (part of the Daren Cilau System)

Location   The cave is situated in the Clydach Gorge approximately halfway between Devils Bridge and the obvious rising of Pwll-y-Cwm. The entrance is in the north bank behind a fallen Elm tree.

Description   Although of short length (only the first 70 m is accessible to non-divers) the cave is quite arduous and constricted in one place. It is however an important site as it provides an underwater connection to Pwll-y-Cwm and the downstream end of the Daren Cilau system.

A squeeze through the top of the keyhole shaped entrance enters a rift high enough to stand in. From here a pool leads under a rock arch to an uncomfortable crawl between vertically bedded rock. After a short distance, a roomie; Z-bend leads to a continuation of the crawl which becomes very tight. Beyond is a T-junction. To the right quickly reaches a sump while to the left, two ducks lead to a rift which ends at a deep gravel pool. **THIS SUMP HAS BEEN DIVED FOR 43 M IN A CONSTRICTED PASSAGE TO EMERGE IN A LARGE UNDERWATER PASSAGE AT A DEPTH OF 15 M. DOWNSTREAM THE PASSAGE REACHES THE BOTTOM**

Paul Taylor in the streamway Ogof Ffynnon Ddu 2

The Cloud Chamber, Dan-yr-C

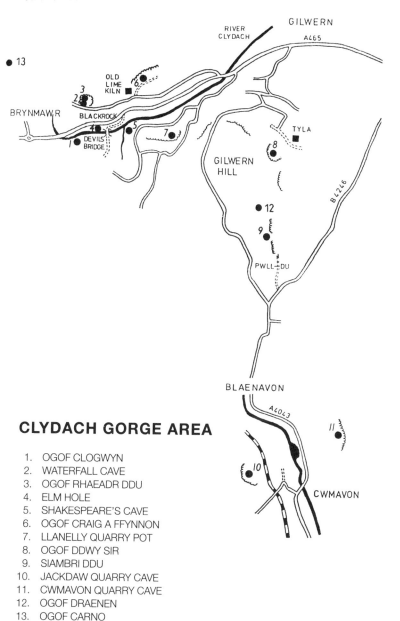

CLYDACH GORGE AREA

1. OGOF CLOGWYN
2. WATERFALL CAVE
3. OGOF RHAEADR DDU
4. ELM HOLE
5. SHAKESPEARE'S CAVE
6. OGOF CRAIG A FFYNNON
7. LLANELLY QUARRY POT
8. OGOF DDWY SIR
9. SIAMBRI DDU
10. JACKDAW QUARRY CAVE
11. CWMAVON QUARRY CAVE
12. OGOF DRAENEN
13. OGOF CARNO

OF PWLL-Y-CWM AFTER 27 M. UPSTREAM THE PASSAGE SURFACES AT THE TERMINAL SUMP IN DAREN CILAU AFTER ABOUT 600 M.
History   First explored by HCC in 1961. Connection with Daren Cilau made by CDG in 1986. Survey in CSS Records (19) 1992.

Jackdaw Quarry Cave No.1   Grade 4

Grid Ref SO2663 0693 OS Maps 1:50 000 sheet 161, 1:25 000 sheet SO/20	
Altitude: 306 metres	
Length: 73 metres	

Location   The cave is situated in a disused quarry in Cwm Afon on the opposite side of the valley to Cwmavon Quarry Cave. Take the A4043 from Blaenavon towards Pontypool and then take the first turning right after the Cwmavon reservoir. The road passes over an iron railway bridge near the old Cwmavon station. By following the railway track northwards for about 400 m or so, the quarry is reached on the left hand side of the track. The entrance to the cave is situated on the nose of the central buttress about 12 m down from the top. A handline is required to descend a slope to the edge of the cliff face from where a ladder or rope is required to reach the entrance.
Description   A fairly short cave which has been extensively dug. There are a lot of loose rocks in the final section of the cave and care must be taken.
A dry and sandy solution tube which is about 1 m in diameter leads after about 5 m to a rift pot in the floor. The pot is 4.5 m deep but there is no way on at the bottom. The way on is across the top of the pot to a small chamber. By squeezing through boulders and climbing down in the left-hand corner of the chamber another crawl is entered which leads to a climb up into another chamber. A short excavated crawl then leads to the top of a 13 m deep pot which can be descended using a handline but which becomes too tight at the bottom.
Tackle   Slope above cliff – 15 m handline
Pitch to Entrance – 9 m rope/ladder, belay and lifeline.
13 m Pot – 15 m handline
History   Survey by Llanelly Diggers 1990.

Jackdaw Quarry Pot   Grade 4

Grid Ref SO2663 0693 OS Maps 1:50000 sheet 161,	
1:25000 Brecon Beacons Eastern O/L	
Altitude : 312 metres	
Length : 33 metres	
Vertical Range : 23 metres	

Location   Situated in the same quarry as Jackdaw Quarry Cave. The entrance is an obvious hole at the northern end of the quarry.
Description   A small vertical cave which is not suitable to persons of above average size.
Just inside the entrance the passage lowers to a crawl and doubles back on itself to reach the top of a pitch. This starts as a squeeze dropping into a small cross

passage and then a descent of 8 m in a reasonably roomy pot reaches a landing. From here a further 8 m descent in an ever tightening rift leads to the end of the cave where it becomes too tight for further progress.

Tackle   15 m handline

History   Survey by Llanelly Diggers 1990.

Llanelly Quarry Pot   Grade 4

Grid Ref SO2247 1237   OS Maps 1:50 000 sheet 161,
                                                        1:25 000 Brecon Beacons Eastern O/L

Altitude: 270 metres

Length: 1705 metres
Vertcal Range : 80 metres

Location   Situated in a disused quarry on the south side of the gorge. From the A465, at the bottom of the gorge, take the side road towards the village of Clydach and then take the first turning right and follow the road up the hill towards Daren-felen. A short distance past a viaduct on the left, an old railway arch leads into the quarry. The entrance to the cave is at the far end of the quarry, on the right hand side, and is slightly above the level of the quarry floor.

Description   A sizeable cave with a long streamway, the water reappearing in Shakespeare's Cave lower down in the gorge. The rift near the entrance is very narrow and not passable to persons of above average size. There is danger from loose rocks in the entrance rift and main pitch areas.

The entrance is a short vertical hole which drops into a small passage. The way on is to the left into a deep narrow rift. Descent and ascent of this rift can prove very arduous as there is no room to use either rope or ladder. Halfway down the rift becomes very tight. At the bottom, a small but pleasant streamway meanders past some small formations to the top of a large shaft. *A tricky traverse along the left-hand wall at this point leads to a crawl and 2 m climb to New Year's Day extension and a small inlet.* The shaft is 20 m deep. Belay the lifeline to a plate on the left-hand wall and the ladder to a scaffold pole 3 m down from the top. At the bottom another scaffolded pitch of 4.5m leads to a crawl through boulders into the main streamway.

Upstream, progress is made at stream level in a narrow passage with thin rock shelves and several groups of stals. Occasionally it is necessary to traverse above the water and at one point there is a small waterfall. After some distance the roof lowers to a duck and crawl. Beyond, the passage opens out again in a lofty passage known as Midsummer Night's Dream. This part of the streamway is very well decorated with many small white stals and straws. Near a small formation known as the Totem Pole is an aven. *This is Totem Aven Series and has been climbed for about 40 m with several blind passages going off.* 50 m beyond the Totem Pole the roof again lowers to a draughty 30 m long duck known as Ryans Duck. On the other side is a large fault chamber and by following the stream a boulder choke is reached. A not very obvious crawl on the left-hand wall at the start of the choke soon opens out into the Fault Series. At the end of this small series it is possible to get a good view of the fault, the different beds of rock being easily distinguishable. Back at the choke, crawling and squeezing amongst the boulders leads to a roomy chamber and an impenetrable sump.

Downstream from the base of the shafts, the nature of the passage varies. Again there are many rock shelves and some fine scalloping and the passage meanders erratically. It is necessary to traverse along a high level route for part of the way but eventually the 2 m wide Hammer Passage is reached with a small inlet coming in from the right. Continuing downstream, calcite formations completely block the route and are bypassed by a squeeze down into the stream followed by 20 m of crawling in water. A climb up then leads to the 4.5 m Guillotine Climb into the Midsummer Nights Nightmare Streamway. Although the passage is still quite high, progress becomes increasingly more difficult with difficult traverses with few foot holds and in places it is necessary to crawl in the stream. Eventually a narrow sump is reached which is only a short distance from the upstream end of Shakespeare's Cave.

Tackle First Pitch - 20m rope/ladder, belay and lifeline.
Totem Aven Series - 22 m handline, 3 x 6 m ladders, belays and lifeline plus 12 Petzl bolts and hangers.

History First explored by BNSSS in 1963. Main streamway discovered in 1988 by the Llanelly Diggers after extensive digging operations. Survey Llanelly Diggers 1988-89.

WARNING There are many loose stones and rocks in the first part of the cave. Care should be taken particularly in the entrance rift and main pitch areas.

Ogof Capel   Grade 2

Grid Ref SO2166 1259   OS Maps 1:50 000 sheet 161,
1:25 000 Brecon Beacons Eastern O/L

Altitude: 220 metres

Length: 796 metres

Location The cave is situated in the gorge. From the pedestrian subway, climb the stile and follow a path to the left besides the fence and down a steep slope to an alcove in the cliff containing the obvious entrance to the cave.

Access The cave is gated and access is administered by Bill Gascoine on behalf of the Mynydd Llangatwg CMAC. Keys are available to CDG members by sending a 10 deposit and an SAE to Bill at 18 Groveside Villas, Pontnewynydd, Pontypool, Gwent. NP4 6SZ giving as much notice as possible.

Description Only the first part of the cave is accessible to non-divers.
A normally dry crawl reaches a junction. The right hand branch goes to a dig. Two passages to the left both reach a sump which is only passable by divers. SUMP 1 IS 12 M LONG TO A LARGE AIRBELL. SUMP 2 IS 6 M LONG TO A CHAMBER CONTAINING A BOULDER CHOKE. A ROUTE FOLLOWING THE LEFT HAND WALL REACHES A LOW SECTION OF PASSAGE WHICH ENLARGES ON JOINING A STREAM. A LITTLE WAY BEYOND IS SHRIMP SUMP PASSAGE ON THE LEFT. THE MAIN ROUTE IS WELL DECORATED AND REACHES A JUNCTION WITH SLALOM PASSAGE ON THE RIGHT. SSSFAGTICGWP STREAM PASSAGE CONTINUES AHEAD WITH MANY FORMATIONS TO REACH A DUCK. BEYOND, THE CAVE DEVELOPS INTO A TALL RIFT WHICH EVENTUALLY BECOMES TOO NARROW.

History Extended in 1987 by CCC. Survey in CSS Records (19) 1992.

Ogof Carno   Grade 4
Alternative name : Carno Adit Cave

Grid Ref SO1640 1260   OS Maps 1:50 000 sheet 161,
                                        1:25 000 Brecon Beacons Eastern O/L

Length : 7000 metres +

Location   Situated in a "Welsh Water" tunnel in Cwm Carno, Beaufort, WNW of
Brynmawr and the Clydach Gorge. The grid ref given is for the entrance to the
tunnel.
Access   Access is controlled by Brynmawr Caving Club on behalf of Welsh
Water PLC. Keys are held by eight persons whose names are registered with
Welsh Water and are responsible for the welfare of visiting cavers. Caving trips will
be overseen by the key holders who will open and lock the gate and, where
possible, be inside the cave for the duration of the trip. Visiting cavers are free to
explore providing that they fill in the log book and inform BCC of any finds they
make. There is no restriction on party-size but safe caving practice is insisted
upon.
Trips can be organised by telephoning a key holder and arranging a date and
time. Reasonable notice should be given. Key holders are as follows :- Charles
Bailey (0873 831689), Chris Brady (0873 858451), Phil Coles (0495 301265),
Dave Crompton (0685 70504), Huw Durban (0495 312525), Bill Gascoine (0495
764489), Phil Jayne (0633 873312), and John Jones (0443 875123).
PLEASE NOTE : Welsh Water owns the Adit; the Duke of Beaufort owns the land;
cavers pass through the Adit only with permission from Welsh Water and any
damage or bad behaviour could result in closure.
Description   Ogof Carno is a natural cave opened up by digging in the tunnel. It
is a sporting and demanding cave with many climbs, crawls, and areas of loose
boulders as well as a permanent neck-deep duck. It should only be entered by fit
and experienced cavers with competent leaders.
The entrance to the cave is 1750 m inside the tunnel where a brick-lined hole in
the right hand wall gives access to a rope climb down of 3 m into an excavated
chamber and a 20 m long crawl. A small stream issues from two avens above in
wet weather. The crawl opens out at the head of an 8 m pitch with a fixed ladder
down into a large chamber. *Upstream ends at a boulder choke* but the way on is
downstream in a wet rift. The rift contains a neck-deep duck and several metres
of wading in water before ending at a T-junction and a climb to the right into a
crawl over a knobbly limestone floor (Spongework Passage).
This leads to a climb up on the left into a continuation of the rift and a vertical
drop down of 3 m into a mud-floored stooping sized passage (Greasy Pot). A
chamber follows and a series of crawls and climbs lead to another chamber with
a large sandbank on the right (Dune Chamber). In wet weather the cave can flood
to this point rendering the passages almost totally sumped for over 100 m; the
floods can be sudden and longlasting and their character is not yet fully
understood.
Beyond Dune Chamber is another chamber and a climb up on the right leads to a
stooping passage which goes over a 15 m deep rift before opening out at the
head of an 8 m pitch (Silo Pitch). This also has a fixed ladder and, at the
bottom,the way on is through a crawling and stooping sand-floored passage.
Also at the foot of Silo Pitch, access can be gained to a deep mud-lined shaft,

OGOF CARNO

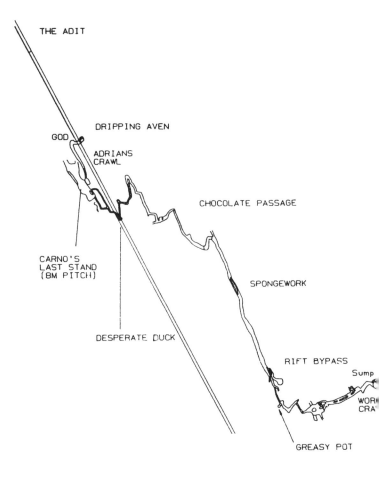

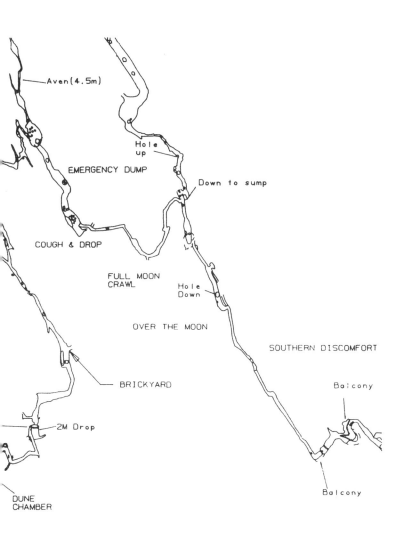

Aven(4.5m)

Hole up

EMERGENCY DUMP

Down to sump

COUGH & DROP

FULL MOON CRAWL

Hole Down

OVER THE MOON

SOUTHERN DISCOMFORT

BRICKYARD

Balcony

2M Drop

DUNE CHAMBER

Balcony

Based on surveys by C.S.S. & B.C.C.

but entry must be done with care. Climbing out is very difficult and no way on from the bottom has been pushed to date.

The sand-floored passage leads to a small boulder-strewn chamber with a large aven in its roof, The Brickyard. Straight on, a hands and knees crawl continues for many metres to the head of a large rift called Pandoras Pot. *This is 20 m deep and leads to a short section of small stream passage and a sump.* The main way on however, is over the top of Pandoras into a continuation of the crawl. This leads to a 4 m climb down followed by several other small climbs up and down in twisting crawls and rifts; route finding can be difficult in this area. Eventually the passage opens out into a large sandy canyon and an equipment dump; food, water, sleeping bags, and first-aid kits are stored here for "flooded-in" cavers and for rescue; please do not use !

Just before the dump, a climb up in the rift gives access to Frightnight Series, climbs, crawls, rifts and avens heading northwestwards.

Beyond the dump, the passage ends at a boulder choke (Cough and Drop), but a climb down below the floor leads to a 70 m crawl, Full Moon Crawl, which is very tight in places. *The crawl has a large aven in its roof after 40 m which can be climbed into an ascending passage and a large chamber called Dark-side Chamber. This is "Over The Moon Series", and a series of climbs up and down in rifts and crawls eventually leads back to the head of the large aven above the Brickyard.*

Straight on in Full Moon Crawl for a further 30 m leads to a major junction, with a series of large passages going off southeastwards and northwestwards at different levels.

To the northwest, two passages (Upstairs and Downstairs), can be followed until they join at Whale Chamber; some calcite formations can be found in this area of the cave. *Above Whale Chamber, a climb up a fixed rope leads into The Blowhole, a series of small sandy rifts and canyons and a large chamber known as Deathwish 6.* Straight on from Whale Chamber leads to the Northern Choke and the Selenite Rift Series. A fixed rope hangs on a difficult rift climb down and there are several tight squeezes and loose boulders to be negotiated. A route through a boulder choke at the end of Selenite Rift Series leads to a large passage, Car Crusher Passage, which continues the trend northwest. At the far end, a section of tight and tortuous passage leads to Car Crusher North, a lofty sandy-floored passage about 150 m long. At the end a boulder choke gives access to True Grit, a series of small muddy passages and chambers leading to a large canyon passage which ends at an aven and another boulder choke.

Back at the end of Full Moon Crawl, two passages head southeast; *firstly down a pot in the floor, Apollo Pot, which gives access to a section of stream passage, a short sump and a series of large muddy chambers which can also be entered from a crawl on the left of Downstairs Passage just before the "big stuff",* and secondly, up a large boulder floored rift, Southern Discomfort.

Southern Discomfort is a large muddy rift which gets muddier and more difficult as you progress. After around 400 m, a climb up on the left leads to a junction with passages going southeast (Open Season Series) and north (Precious Years Series).

The Open Season Series is an extensive series of large and small passages trending in a generally southeasterly direction. There are copious amounts of mud and at present ends in sumps.

The northern series, Precious Years, is even more extensive and is entered via a 2 m drop into a large passage which is followed to a wide breakdown chamber. A way through the boulders on the right hand wall leads via a series of crawls and stooping passages to a lofty inclined rift. A squeeze between boulders and a drop through a slot in the floor then leads to a tighter and more awkward rift which gradually increase in size. The single passage continues via several small climbs to a junction, Crossways.

The main way on from Crossways increases in size and the passage is followed via Pillar Hall to Pinnacle Corner, a sharp left turn with a rock pinnacle on the floor. *A climb between Pillar Hall and Pinnacle Corner leads up into a very large chamber with a natural rock bridge, Green Bridge Cavern, and a series of large fossil passages.* The main passage continues from Pinnacle Corner and is smaller than before, eventually becoming a crawl with a drop into a passage ending at a sump, "C" Sump. **THIS SUMP HAS BEEN DIVED FOR 18 M INTO SEVERAL HUNDRED METRES OF TIGHT AND UNPLEASANT STREAMWAY WITH AN INCONCLUSIVE END.**

History Originally discovered in 1982 by Bill Gascoine and Steve Pedrazzoli. Major extensions made from 1991 onwards and exploration is still going on. Survey 1992, Descent (106)

WARNING : THE CAVE IS LIABLE TO FLOODING.

Ogof Clogwyn   Grade 2

Grid Ref SO2129 1238 OS Maps 1:50 000 sheet 161,	
	1:25 000 Brecon Beacons Eastern O/L
Altitude: 235 metres	
Length: 352 metres	

Location The cave is situated in the gorge. Follow the river upstream from Devil's Bridge for about 400 m, then a climb up the bank on the left leads to the foot of a cliff about 6 m above the river. The entrance to the cave is in the cliff face and a small stream usually issues from the opening.

Description A small but interesting cave which contains some fine examples of phreatic rock shelving. It is also a good cave for beginners.

The main entrance is above a small overhanging lip which can be ascended without too much difficulty. There are two more very tight entrances to the right. The entrance leads directly to an active stream passage with some fine rock shelves. The water is quite deep in places but is easily traversed over using the shelves. The passage continues for some distance until the roof lowers to meet the water at a sump. A few metres before the main sump, a crawl low down on the right hand wall can be followed to another smaller sump.

At one of the right-angled turns in the streamway a high level muddy passage can be followed back towards the cliff face where daylight can be seen through an impenetrable crack. The passage then turns right and becomes larger but soon ends. By staying low at the start of this high level passage a crawl can be followed to the left to a hole in the roof of the main streamway further downstream.

History The cave has probably been known for a long time but the first recorded exploration was by the SWCC. Survey in CSS Records (19) 1992.

Ogof Craig-a-Ffynnon   Grade 4
Alternative name: Rock & Fountain Cave

Grid Ref SO2201 1286   OS Maps 1:50 000 sheet 161,
                                          1:25 000 Brecon Beacons Eastern O/L

Altitude: 255 metres

Length: 12800 metres

Location   The entrance to the cave is situated on the north-western side of the
gorge in old quarry workings directly above the Rock & Fountain Inn.
Access   The cave is on private land owned by the Duke of Beaufort's Estates and
access has been entrusted to Grwp Ogoffydd Craig-a-Ffynnon. Applications for
trips should be made to Jeff Hill, 11 York Avenue, Ebbw Vale, Gwent NP3 6US.
Description   A large cave which penetrates deep into the Llangattock mountain
and comes close to parts of the Daren Cilau system. Throughout its entire length
the cave is well decorated with both calcite formations and laminated mud banks.
Routes through much of the cave have been taped to avoid any unnecessary
damage. ALL PARTIES MUST FOLLOW THESE ROUTES AND NOT CROSS
THE TAPES.
The entrance passage which is an excavated crawl gives access after about 60
m to a series of well decorated chambers. The stream passage, which floods to
the roof in wet weather, is then followed until the First Boulder Choke is reached.
The way through is via a series of fixed steel ladders and scaffolding poles which
are preventing the choke from collapsing. On the other side of the choke is a
large chamber with many mud formations. The way on is by way of a crawl in a
gravel bottomed stream passage called Gascoline Alley. After a further 91 m the
North West Inlet is reached. *To the left, a 9 m long tunnel gives access to a
stream passage, Things to Come Passage, which is over 500 m long. It
becomes progressively larger upstream and contains many fine formations,
ending in a boulder choke. In wet weather the initial 90 m of this passage is
liable to severe flooding and should only be entered in settled conditions.*
By going to the right at North West Inlet, a walking sized passage leads to a 5 m
long flat-out crawl over flowstone and then a 12 m aven. This aven leads to the
Second Boulder Choke which has recently collapsed but has now been
reopened and care is needed. It is generally arduous and uncomfortable and
leads to a series of large dry fossil galleries containing many formations and large
mud banks. This continues for over 500 m to the Third Boulder Choke which is
immediately after the impressive 28 m high Hall of the Mountain Kings. *A
passage found to the right of the Hall of the Mountain Kings as you enter, can
be followed eastwards for about 200 m.* The main way on is at the bottom right
hand side of the choke, along a flat-out crawl for about 12 m. Beyond this is
nearly 250 m of hands and knees crawl, Hurricane Highway, which then leads to
a long straight phreatic canyon called Severn Tunnel. This is turn leads to Severn
Tunnel Junction where several large dry passages join.
*Straight on and to the left leads to a series of passages, all of which end in
boulder chokes.* The right hand passage slopes downwards to a rift in the floor.
*A 15 m climb down the rift leads to a stream passage, Blaen Elin, which can
be followed for about 120 m downstream to a boulder choke. This stream has
been dye tested to Things to Come Passage.* By carrying on over the top of the
rift the main way on is followed via a large boulder ruckle to the Fourth Boulder

Choke. *Immediately prior to the Fourth Choke, a small passage on the left gives access to the Lower Series. An awkward 6 m climb on the right of a high sandy chamber leads to a 15 m deep pot with a narrow high rift at the bottom. This then leads to a series of well decorated grottoes. A stream passage can be reached by dropping 5 m down a sandy pitch.*

Upstream and downstream is tight and slippery and both directions end in boulder chokes. Great care must be taken to avoid touching the formations, particularly in the part known as Isadora's Grotto, as access to the 5 m pot is only gained by picking ones way carefully through the decorations.

The way through the Fourth Boulder Choke is via an excavated crawl on the right where great care should be taken due to the instability of the area. Beyond is a continuation of the large passage which ends after a little more than 200 m at the Fifth Boulder Choke which has not been passed. *Just over halfway along this passage is a 6 m pitch on the left which drops into another lower stream passage which can be followed downstream for about 120 m to a well decorated chamber and a boulder choke. The upstream passage, called the Promised Land, gives access to nearly 1200 m of mainly large passage which ends in an area of collapse.*

History   Discovered by J.Parker and J.Hill after a long dig. Survey GOCAF.
WARNING :   THE CAVE IS LIABLE TO FLOOD. The stream passage near the entrance can flood to the roof in wet weather.

Ogof Ddwy Sir   Grade 1

Grid Ref SO2450 1280   OS Maps 1:50 000 sheet 161,
                                          1:25 000 Brecon Beacons Eastern O/L

Altitude: 381 metres

Length: 140 metres

Location   The cave is situated in Quimps Quarry on Gilwern Hill to the south of the gorge. It is the third quarry round starting from Clydach but is best approached by taking the single track road to Tyla (marked on 1:25 000 OS maps) and then climbing straight up the hillside.

Description   A simple cave consisting of a single passage for almost its entire length. The cave is exceptionally dry throughout.

The entrance is a narrow rift about 2 m high and is easily spotted. This gives access to a passage in very shattered rock. After about 25 m, a low squeeze leads into a more stable area and the passage become higher and narrower. In several places it is necessary to climb up into the roof over boulders. The passage ends in a mud choke and just before this is the only side passage which becomes too tight after only a very short distance.

History   First recorded exploration was by SWCC in 1951.

Ogof Draenen

Grade 4/5

Grid Ref SO 2463 1178   OS Maps 1:50 000 sheet 161,
1:25 000 Brecon Beacons Eastern O/L

Altitude : 362 metres

Length : 28,000 metres +

Location When approaching from Blaenavon, take a left turn at Keeper's Pond. The first building on the right is the Lamb & Fox pub. Park opposite the pub on an area of concrete. Continue down the road and cross the stile immediately to the north of the Pwll Du Adventure Centre. Follow the fence you've just crossed down a steep slope until you reach a small stream. From here an obvious path leads directly to the entrance.

Access   The cave is gated, for information about access contact Tim Long, 4 Brynllefrith Cottages, Llantrisant Road, Llantwit Fardre, Mid Glamorgan, CF38 2HD, enclosing a stamped self-addressed envelope. Visitors are requested to observe any taping and treat bats with the respect they deserve.

Description   Ogof Draenen is one of the largest caves in Britain. It offers a great variety of caving and some very spectacular sights. The cave should not be underestimated and the round trip should be treated very seriously.

The entrance dig drops into a low crawl where there is a gate. Beyond the gate, a hole on the right leads down to a low, wet, bedding plane crawl, which emerges in a boulder choke. A squeeze down through the choke (care is required) reaches the top of an 8m scaffolded shaft. This was the break through point and emerges in a small chamber. *Straight on are Darling Rifts, which lead to Big Bang Pitch and the original Pitch Bypass.* However, an easier route is to duck under the right hand wall, into Spare Rib. Dropping down a slot on the left, leads to an inlet which can be followed down a cascade, to a chamber where the original Pitch Bypass rejoins. A low passage on the right leads via a 5m climb down to Cairn Junction, in the impressive main passage: Beyond A Choke.

From Cairn Junction, *left leads to the bottom of Big Bang Pitch and a section of streamway fed from sinks on Gilwern Hill,* whereas right leads to Tea Junction. To get to Tea Junction from Cairn Junction, either follow the main passage, or taking the first left turning after Cairn Junction, which enters WonderBra Bypass. Descending a hole on the right a short way along WonderBra Bypass, leads back to the main streamway just upstream of Tea Junction. At Tea Junction, the sizeable White Arch Passage enters on the left and to the right is the continuation of Beyond A Choke.

Climbing a short slope on the right, 50m downstream of Tea Junction, enters Gilwern Passage, which can be followed for 700m, via some superb formations (Great Care Required), to a choke. Up the choke leads to Old Illtydian's Chamber on the left and Morgannwg Passage on the right. Morgannwg Passage has been taped off due to the very delicate formations it contains and is therefore out of bounds. At the end of Gilwern Passage the water can be followed into a choke, which leads into Galeria Garimpeiros, a fine section of passage which in turn leads via a low duck into the St Giles Extensions.

From Tea Junction, Beyond A Choke is 2.5km of uninterrupted streamway - probably the longest in Britain. It can be followed downstream via a number of cascades to two chokes (30m apart). *Just before the chokes a 13m climb and difficult traverse leads to The Score.* Each choke can be passed by climbing out

OGOF DRAENEN

Based on a survey by Morgannwg C.C.

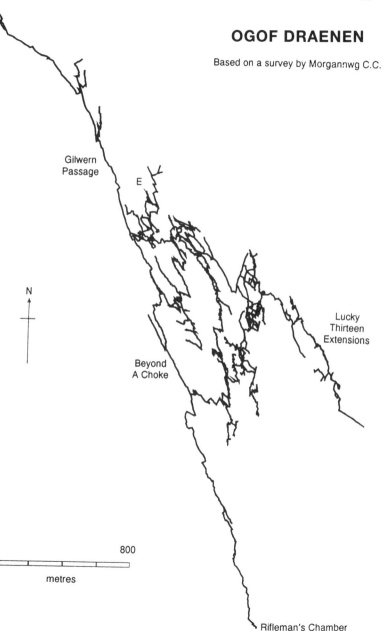

Gilwern Passage

E

N

Lucky Thirteen Extensions

Beyond A Choke

800

metres

Rifleman's Chamber

of the streamway and squeezing between boulders on the right, where another squeeze leads back to the streamway. Beyond the chokes, Agent Blorenge inlet enters from the left. The main streamway continues through some sections of chest deep wading for a further 1.3km, to the present limit of exploration at Rifleman's Chamber.

Back at Tea Junction, White Arch Passage can be followed for 500m to a choke. A crawl in the top right hand corner leads into the impressive Lamb & Fox Chamber. High up in the chamber on the right hand side, a climb up a boulder slope leads to Indiana Highway. *After a short distance a bedding plane at floor level leads to Raiders Passage on the right and back to Lamb & Fox Chamber on the left.* A long section of fine traverses, including an exposed section over a 20m pitch, leads to a junction. To the right is The Canyon, but the way on is to the left and up over boulders on to a ledge above a trench in the floor. Following the trench left leads in to Mega Drive North (which loops round to connect with The Canyon), but the way on is immediately right into Mega Drive. This is followed for some distance to a sharp left bend immediately before Windy Junction. *To the right is Going Square,* but continuing ahead is The Nunnery, which passes Perseverance II, Perseverance I and then terminates in The Chapel.

At the first junction in The Nunnery, turning right along Perseverance II (a crawl over cobbles) leads to a junction. Sharp right leads to the very tall Fault Chambers, which lead to Fault Rifts and a connection with Going Square. The large passage leaving the first chamber is Eliptic Passage, leading to the Lucky Thirteen Extensions. Straight on leads to the 8m Balcony Pitch over looking The Arms Park. From the bottom of the pitch the way on is to left into The Players' Tunnel, two other passages also leave the chamber, a climb with a cord on it leads up into Erection Series and Players' Tunnel North can be followed to a choke. After a short distance down Players' Tunnel it is necessary to drop down through boulders on the left hand side. The passage is now 3m high and 8m wide and is followed via a choke, to another impressive chamber with a perfectly flat roof called St. David's Hall. A small hole in the top left hand wall of the chamber leads into the complicated Squirrel Rifts. The main passage through this area must be followed for a long way, past numerous side passages and junctions, until a sharp right hand turn leads into a reasonably large chamber. *To the right is Wooden Spoon,* but to the left is the Round Trip Connection, which soon lowers to a stooping passage. Soon the passage enters the top of a rift, Traversing out and then dropping down, reaches a 5m climb down into a tight rift making the round trip connection to Haggis Basher One. Left can be followed to a choke, but turning right leads to a slope up on the left, *which leads to the Life On Mars Series,* whereas straight on leads to the Far Agent Blorenge steamway. Upstream quickly leads to a sump but downstream is followed in large passage for 500m to a mud slope leading to a chamber. *Straight ahead is a bedding plane crawl which leads to a junction on the left into Crystal Maze, before rejoining Agent Blorenge.* A shorter way is to follow the water down a rift, this marks the start of the very sporting Agent Blorenge Inlet which feeds into the main Beyond A Choke streamway. Agent Blorenge is followed downstream to a waterfall. *Traversing over the waterfall also leads to Crystal Maze,* but descending the waterfall through a hole in the left wall, drops into The Sewer. This is followed by some tight traversing in a rift which eventually leads to the top of two awkward climbs, care is required here. The way on is either through a duck or up a climb immediately before the duck into a small chamber. The water is then followed for 400m, down several cascades and waterfalls to the main

Beyond A Choke streamway, just down stream of the chokes. Upstream leads back to Tea Junction whereas dowstream leads to Rifleman's Chamber.
Tackle   Balcony Pitch – 25ft ladder, belay and lifeline.
         Big Bang Pitch – 60ft ladder, belay and lifeline.
At the time of writing Balcony Pitch is permanantly rigged.
History   First explored and surveyed by members of Morgannwg CC, after an extensive dig. Major extensions made by several other clubs. Survey - Grade 2/3 available Summer '95, Grade 5 in progress.
WARNING :   THE BEYOND A CHOKE STREAMWAY CAN BECOME VERY SERIOUS AFTER VERY HEAVY RAIN.

Ogof Nant Rhin   Grade 4

Grid Ref SO2104 1242 OS Maps 1:50 000 sheet 161,	
	1:25 000 Brecon Beacons Central O/L

Altitude : 250 metres

Length : 346 metres

Location   Situated in the gorge. From the large layby on the Heads of the Valley Road (A465), scramble down the bank towards the river, trending downstream. The entrance is situated in an unstable scree slope 2 m above the river.
Description   An active resurgence cave containing many fine calcite formations but totally inaccessible to anyone of larger than average build.
An extremely tight and wet crawl emerges into a pool in a hands and knees sized passage containing a small stream, the Nitty Gritty Mississippi. Downstream is blocked immediately and the way on is upstream for 80 m until a chamber with a small waterfall is reached. From here there are two ways on.
Just before the chamber, a climb up into the roof gives access to an inlet passage reached by carefully crawling under straws. This narrow rift passage contains many layers of phreatic shelving and is traversed at various levels until it emerges after 45 m through a squeeze into the large Aven d'Oznog, containing a fine flowstone formation.
Back at the chamber, the main way on is up the waterfall, up phreatic shelving, then dropping back to stream level. A junction is soon reached. *Straight on is a well decorated inlet passage ending in the Garden of Delights, a muddy chamber full of broken stal.*
The way on is to the left, in walking sized passage past a large formation to a chamber. A crawl through fallen roof blocks rejoins the stream. A hands and knees crawl then leads to Distant Voices Aven. The stream is followed through more crawls eventually emerging in Shaven Aven which has been climbed but becomes too tight after 20 m.
The way on is at the far side of the aven, through a short crawl to a tight T-junction. *To the left emerges in a chamber and an area of loose wet rocks.* To the right leads via an awkward flat-out bedding to a junction. Straight on leads through a very tight squeeze to a short stooping passage ending in a chamber, while to the left the passage quickly chokes.
History   First explored in 1991. Survey T.Copeland et al 1993, Descent (111)

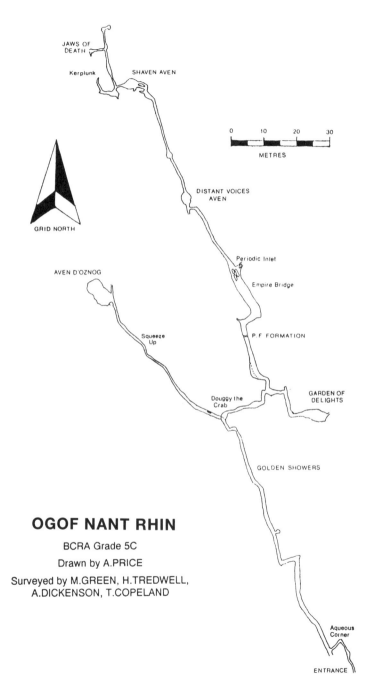

JAWS OF
DEATH

Kerplunk

SHAVEN AVEN

0   10   20   30

METRES

DISTANT VOICES
AVEN

Periodic Inlet

Empire Bridge

AVEN D'OZNOG

Squeeze
Up

P.F FORMATION

Douggy the
Crab

GARDEN OF
DELIGHTS

GRID NORTH

GOLDEN SHOWERS

OGOF NANT RHIN

BCRA Grade 5C

Drawn by A.PRICE

Surveyed by M.GREEN, H.TREDWELL,
A.DICKENSON, T.COPELAND

Aqueous
Corner

ENTRANCE

Ogof Rhaeadr Ddu   Grade 4

Grid Ref SO2120 1250   OS Maps 1:50 000 sheet 161,
                                            1:25 000 Brecon Beacons Eastern O/L

Altitude: 246 metres

Length: 304 metres approx.

Location   Situated in the disused Blackrock Quarry on the minor road which
runs along the northern side of the A465 through the Clydach Gorge. The quarry
is to the right of the road going uphill. The entrance is directly opposite Waterfall
Cave of which it was once a part. A small stream issues from the entrance.
Description   This is a cave which is wet and tight throughout its length.
A narrow rift leads to a small chamber aptly named The Coffin where a large
boulder forms the roof. A very tight crawl is followed until you have to drop down
into the stream. A little further and a climb up a small waterfall gives access to a
high level tube. Follow the passage past an oxbow on the left and then through
two right-angled bends, first to the left and then to the right. A drop back into the
stream and an awkward duck then leads into a high rift passage. The way on is
to climb up into the roof and crawl along a small tube that leads above a second
waterfall.
Directly above the waterfall, a small pot is found in the crawl and a second pot
drops back into the stream. A tight squeeze then leads to a more roomy passage
and the Twin Avens. An 8 m climb up the first aven and a traverse along a ledge
leads to a continuation of the streamway. After about 23 m, the passage turns
sharp right and *Bedroom Oxbow can be entered on the left.* Continuing up the
stream leads to a cross rift and a third high aven on the right. This aven has been
climbed for 40 m and ends in a choke close to the surface.
History   Discovered by BNSSS in 1961. Extended by CCC and CSS in 1980's.
Terminal aven climbed to its end in 1990. Survey in CSS Records (19) 1992.

Pwll y Cwm

Grid Ref SO2150 1250   OS Maps 1:50 000 sheet 161,
                                            1:25 000 Brecon Beacons Eastern O/L

Location   Situated in the Clydach Gorge in the bed of the river near Elm Hole.
Description   This is an important speleological site being the resurgence for the
water originating from the Llangattock caves. It is accessible only to divers and
provides access to the submerged passages leading to Daren Cilau's terminal
sump. It may also provide a way into the main drain from Agen Allwedd.
History   The underwater choke was finally passed in 1993 by Duncan Price.
Survey CSS & CDG 1993, Descent (115)

Shakespeare's Cave   Grade 3/4

Grid Ref SO2170 1249   OS Maps 1:50000 sheet 161,
                                              1:25000 Brecon Beacons Eastern O/L

Altitude: 206 metres

Length: 365 metres

Location   The cave is situated in the gorge downstream from Devil's Bridge.
From the bridge, follow the track above the steep sided gully until it descends to
river level and a stream joins the river from a small valley on the right. The
entrance to the cave is about 50 m up this valley, at the base of a cliff on the left-
hand side. A small stream issues from the cave.
Description   An active and very sporting cave offering some difficulties and a
thorough soaking even in summer. The water in this cave originates in Llanelly
Quarry Pot.
The low entrance leads to a small chamber with the stream issuing from a narrow
rift on the right. The way on is along the rift and upstream for about 75 m to a
duck. Beyond this the passage continues narrow to another duck and then to a
sump. The sump can be free-dived and is about 2 m long with narrow airspace
on the other side and is followed immediately by a duck. A line goes through the
sump and on through the duck.
The sump can be bypassed via a dry crawl which goes off to the right of the
streamway a few metres before reaching the sump. At the end of the crawl, an
awkward tight duck on the left leads back into the stream. The duck is best
passed on one's back. Beyond the duck, the passage straight ahead leads to the
upstream side of the sump but the way on is an immediate turn right by a rock
flake. The passage continues upstream for some distance until it narrows right
down in deep water. Progress along the tight rift becomes impossible and falling
water can be heard through the impassable crack ahead. This point is only a
short distance from the downstream end of Llanelly Quarry Pot.
Tackle   A wet suit is essential.
History   Survey by CSS/ACG.
WARNING: THE CAVE IS LIABLE TO FLOOD.

Siambri Ddu   Grade 1
Alternative name: Black Cavern

Grid Ref SO2509 1145   OS Maps 1:50 000 sheet 161, 1:25 000 sheet SO/12

Length: 45 metres

Location   Situated in Pwll Ddu quarry to the south of the gorge. It is best
approached from the B4246 near Pen-ffordd-goch Pond. A track, marked as a
public footpath, leads to the quarry. The entrance to the cave is in the top bench
of the quarry just before a stone wall.
Description   A short but interesting cave consisting mainly of a huge chamber
lying just below the surface of the moor.
The entrance leads to a crawl on the right and a low squeeze. Beyond the
squeeze, the crawl takes a right-angled turn to emerge in a huge chamber. The
floor of the chamber is littered with boulders and there are many fossils in the roof

and on the floor. There are a few calcite formations at the far end. There is no way on from the chamber.

Waterfall Cave   Grade 3

Grid Ref SO2124 1251   OS Maps 1:50 000 sheet 161,
                                        1:25 000 Brecon Beacons Eastern O/L

Altitude: 244 metres

Length: 105 metres

Location   The cave is situated in the SW corner of the disused Blackrock Quarry on the minor road which runs along the northern side of the A465 through the Clydach Gorge. The quarry is a little to the west of the Drum and Monkey Inn and on the right of the road going uphill towards Brynmawr. A stream runs across the quarry floor from Ogof Rhaeadr Ddu and sinks into the cave.
Description   The small entrance leads immediately into an active stream passage. The passage is small and movement is made difficult by the razor sharp rock. This uncomfortable crawl is followed, over three small cascades (or waterfalls), to an awkward drop of just over 2 m into a large chamber of boulders. By passing through the boulder choke on the left, an area of low collapsed chambers can be entered. A scramble over boulders then leads to the final collapsed chamber and the terminal boulder choke.
History   The cave was first explored by BNSSS in the early 1960's. Surveyed by BNSSS in 1960's. Recent survey in CSS Records (19) 1992.

Lesser Caves and Sites of Speleological Interest

Beech Tree Cave   SO2152 1240
Clydach Springs   SO2149 1244
Dead Dog Cave   SO2212 1328
Devil's Bridge Cave   SO2150 1246
Ffynnon Gisfaen Resurgence   SO2074 1240
Fiddy's Farm Cave   SO279 073
Flood Rising   SO2158 1241
Jackdaw Quarry Cave No.2   SO266 068
Limekiln Quarry Pot   SO2720 0308
Moth Cave   SO2469 1240
Ogof Dial Pridd   SO2772 0606
Overhang Cave   SO2120 1243
Pwll Coedog   SO2141 1327 (doline)
Pwll Ddu Quarry Caves   SO247 125
Pylon Cave   SO2126 1241
Quimps Quarry Caves   SO2436 1284
Rock & Fountain Spring   SO2201 1286

3.   Llangattock Escarpment

Agen Allwedd   Grade 3/5
Alternative name: Keyhole Cave

Grid Ref SO1876 1589   OS Maps 1:50 000 sheet 161,
                                          1:25 000 Brecon Beacons Eastern O/L

Altitude: 366 metres

Length: 32,000 metres approx.

Location   From Brynmawr follow the road which leads over the top of the
Clydach Gorge to the quarries on the Llangattock escarpment. At the point
where the road starts to descend towards Crickhowell, a track straight ahead
continues past the CSS hut (Whitewalls) and along the old tramroad which carries
on around the escarpment into the Craig-y-Cilau Nature Reserve. The present
entrance is via Ogof Gam (Crooked Cave) which is at the base of a cliff to the left
at the very end of the track. The original Agen Allwedd entrance is on a ledge
further along the cliff and a little higher up. Both entrances are gated. Parking is
available in a car park situated near to the Daren Cilau quarry, 400 m from
Whitewalls on the road to Brynmawr.

Access   Entry is controlled by a cave management committee on behalf of the
Countryside Council for Wales. Permits to enter the cave are available to bone
fide caving organisations. Applications should be sent to the Permit Secretary,
Mrs.D.Gascoine, 18 Groveside Villas, Pontnewynedd, Pontypool, Gwent NP4
6SZ enclosing an SAE. At least two weeks notice is required and a 10 deposit is
payable on the key. Only electric lighting is allowed in the cave. Full conditions
and entry procedures are available from the Permit Secretary.

Description   Agen Allwedd is one of the longest caves in Britain. A great deal of
its length is made up of long sections of streamway and large, mainly dry
passages. Although the bulk of the cave presents little technical difficulty, its shear
size and repetitive nature can prove tiring. Despite this, the cave has a number of
interesting features and boasts several lengthy round trips which make it well
worth a visit.

The low entrance leads to a narrow meandering rift and two flat out squeezes.
Soon after, a small stream *from Purgatory Passage straight ahead* joins the
entrance stream to flow down a short crawl under the left hand wall. Keeping left
at all junctions, the passage dimensions gradually increase as two more inlets,
Stream Passage and Queer Street join from the right. The main route leads
directly to the First Boulder Choke. This is passed firstly at high level and then by
dropping back into the lower level through a small hole between boulders near
the right hand wall. A further hole down or switch back down a boulder slope and
under a crawl *past the start of Draught Passage on the right* leads back to the
streamway. This is followed to a crawl under boulders and up a well-worn climb
into the bedding plane and the start of the large Baron's Chamber.

MAIN PASSAGE
Descending the mud and boulder floor of Baron's Chamber leads to the start of
Main Passage which is nearly 1200 m long. After a short distance an obvious
hole down to the right leads to Main Stream Passage as Main Passage continues

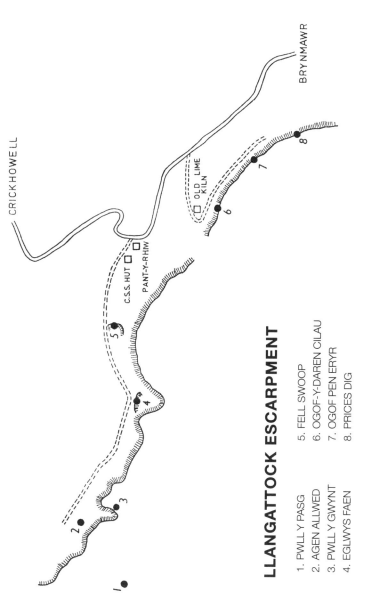

LLANGATTOCK ESCARPMENT

1. PWLL Y PASG
2. AGEN ALLWED
3. PWLL Y GWYNT
4. EGLWYS FAEN

5. FELL SWOOP
6. OGOF-Y-DAREN CILAU
7. OGOF PEN ERYR
8. PRICES DIG

up a steep mud slope straight ahead *passing the entrance to Erse Passage which is also on the right.* There are selenite crystals growing from the floor in several places and these should be viewed from beyond the tapes. *Half way along the passage, the dimensions increase dramatically at the entrance to Southern Stream Passage and Northern Stream Passage down a boulder slope to the right.* Beyond this point the passage height lowers, *passing the start of Trident Passage on the right.* Main Passage continues to the Music Hall and the Cliffs of Dover. A sandy crawl over these mud 'cliffs' gains the North Wing and Aven Series entered through a small hole on the right hand wall.

MAIN STREAM PASSAGE

From Main Passage, a mud slope leads into Main Stream Passage. *After a short distance the stream is joined by another stream from Meander Passage on the right.* Downstream the passage is fairly wide and littered with boulders, eventually narrowing as it reaches the Second Boulder Choke. Beyond the first section of this choke is a chamber containing a choice of routes. *A climb to the left leads to Midnight Passage and Mud Rose Chamber.* Straight on two climbs lead back down to stream level. The second climb can be bypassed by a traverse to the right affording an easier descent to the stream. A climb up at the end of the stream leads to Mud Rose Chamber from where a hole in the floor is descended back into the stream and a crawl through boulders. Beyond, a climb up leads to Keyhole Chamber. Two routes can then be used to regain the stream; either a traverse to the end of the chamber, then a climb down through a hole at the end, or a direct descent at the start of the traverse. A long section of mostly roomy streamway is then followed to Northwest Junction where a larger stream is met flowing from right to left.

Downstream the passage enlarges *as it is joined by Cascade Passage on the right.* The streamway provides comfortable going for several hundred metres until it enters an area of mudbanks. This is followed by a wade in the stream known as Deep Water and a rift section in out-of-depth water at the Narrows. A swim may be avoided by traversing above the stream. A low arch, which can become a duck in wet weather and sumps in flood, leads to the Third Boulder Choke. A hole part way up the middle of the choke drops back down to stream level. Following the solid left hand wall quickly gains open passage. Climbing over a large rubble slope rejoins the stream which soon disappears into the base of the Fourth Boulder Choke. This is passed by a tight and loose corkscrew climb to a crawl. After 50 m a fork is reached, to the left is Bat Passage, to the right Biza Passage continues as a series of phreatic switchbacks ending at two rope climbs down into the Lower Main Stream Passage.

Upstream the passage quickly reaches the Fifth Boulder Choke. Almost immediately downstream, the water cascades into a wide, deep pool. The pool can either be swum or a loose traverse around the right hand wall is possible with care. The passage continues in fine style passing a large rock fall at Quarry Corner until a second cascade is met. A crawl along a ledge on the right hand wall and a climb back into the stream avoids much of the water. Further downstream, *a fixed rope hanging down the right hand wall marks the climb up into High Traverse Passage* before the roof lowers to a section which can sump in flood. The passage regains some of its former size, *passing the bottom end of Southern Stream Passage* before terminating at a sump in gradually deepening water. **SUMP 1 IS 76 M LONG, INITIALLY SHALLOW, WITH A DROP OFF ON A LEFT-HAND CORNER HALFWAY THROUGH THE DIVE. THIS IS FOLLOWED BY 45 M OF PASSAGE TO**

SUMP 2, 30 M LONG AND SHALLOW. 30 M OF CANAL GAINS SUMP 3. THIS BEGINS AS A GRADUAL DESCENT TO 7 M OVER A SANDY FLOOR AS THE LARGE PASSAGE ZIG-ZAGS BEFORE SURFACING IN MAYTIME AFTER A DIVE OF 270 M. These first three sumps can now be bypassed via High Traverse Passage and Resurrection Passage. After 500 m of stream passage in Maytime, Sump 4 is reached. **THIS IS IN A LARGE PASSAGE WITH ALCOVES AND AFTER 290 M REACHES AGAINST ALL ODDS CHAMBER. THE CHAMBER IS 20 M LONG, UP TO 5 M WIDE AND 5 M HIGH. AT THE END IS A LARGE BOULDER CHOKE 10 M HIGH AND 7 M WIDE. SUMP 5 CONTINUES FROM THE END OF SUMP 4 AND THE WATER IS PRESUMED TO FLOW UNDER THE CHAMBER AND AS YET NO WAY ON HAS BEEN FOUND.**

Upstream from Northwest Junction is known as the Turkey Streamway. Initially narrow, the passage gradually widens to a fine streamway. A few formations are passed including a large beehive. *After 300 m, Coal Cellar Passage leads off to the right at a prominent junction. This starts as a walking sized passage but gradually deteriorates into a narrow rift after passing several side passages on the right. A tight upwards climb at the end of the passage enters Midsummer Passage from behind an obscure boulder.* Turkey Streamway continues straight ahead, *passing the entrance to Shattered Passage and the 1984 Series on the right*, before reaching Turkey Pool which is a narrow rift to the left in deep water. Beyond, the passage changes character but soon a climb up through boulders enters the large Turkey Chamber. Climbing up over the boulder slope to the right and then descending over large boulders leads back to the streamway. This continues past *an obvious side passage to the right, Hawkins Horror which leads to Sand Caverns and the Summertime Series.* Upstream the passage reaches the large Terminal Chamber beneath a high aven after about 600 m. Beyond this point the streamway narrows into a tight rift before reaching a sump which can be bypassed to reach Sump 2 and the beginning of the Remembrance Series by a tight route back to the right. **SUMP 2 IS 27 M LONG AND ONLY PASSABLE BY DIVERS. THIS EMERGES INTO A SHORT SECTION OF STREAMWAY AND HIGH LEVEL PASSAGE WITH A VOCAL CONNECTION TO THE DOWNSTREAM END OF SUMP 2. UPSTREAM, SUMP 3 IS 6 M LONG FOLLOWED BY A SMALL PASSAGE LEADING TO SUMP 4. THIS IS BYPASSED BY A CLIMB UP INTO A HIGH LEVEL PASSAGE WHICH REJOINS THE STREAMWAY NEAR TO SUMP 5. THIS IS BETWEEN 45 AND 70 M LONG DEPENDING ON WATER LEVELS, AND STARTS AS A TIGHT GRAVEL SQUEEZE. REMEMBRANCE PASSAGE CONTINUES TO A JUNCTION WITH NORTHERN INLET AND EASTERN INLET BEFORE PASSING THROUGH A WATERLOGGED CANAL TO TERMINATE IN A SERIES OF AVENS AND BREAKDOWN.**

SUMMERTIME SERIES

From the small entrance off of Turkey Streamway the route enters the large Sand Caverns Passage. *To the left leads to a choke,* but the way on is to the right *passing the entrance to Selenite Needle Passage up a mud bank on the right.* Ahead, the main passage continues *passing the end of Western Avenue up a steep slope to the right,* eventually ending in an area of chokes. Selenite Needle Passage begins as a crawl over mud, enlarging as it meets the ends of *Western Avenue and Central Avenue from the left, both of which lead back to Sand Caverns.* The passage ends at a junction with a stream in the larger Eastern Avenue. Taking the right hand branch enters the large Midsummer Passage. *To the right the passage diminishes in size, passing a low section before enlarging again near to the squeeze down into the end of Coal Cellar Passage behind a block on the right. Beyond this point the route degenerates into a low crawl eventually dividing to end in chokes.* To the left, Midsummer Passage continues big, *passing Shamrock Passage on the left,* to a T-junction. *To the right, Swiss Passage passes some interesting mud formations which resemble an alpine village.* To the left, a choice of routes lead into Scree Passage and the ascent of two rubble slopes to the Dome of St.Pauls. The main passage passes a large inlet to the right, bearing round to the left through Inner Circle Chamber before meeting a junction with a stream. *Upstream leads to a choke,* whilst downstream reaches the junction of Eastern Avenue to the right and Selenite Needle Passage to the left.

SOUTHERN STREAM PASSAGE
From the large entrance off of Main Passage, descend over boulders and through a short climb up and down a mud slope. A hole down to stream level leads to a stooping height passage with much hands and knees crawling and clambering over boulders. *Back in the larger passage the route continues up a slope to Upper Southern Stream Passage and a small tube into Sandstone Passage.* After 140 m the passage meets an inlet on the left. After a further 400 m a second, impenetrable, inlet from the right brings water from Sandstone Passage. Beyond this point the route becomes a series of crawls through water ending at a particularly low section with a squeeze to the left up through boulders. This rejoins the stream as the going gets easier until reaching Waterfall Chamber. A 2 m climb leads to a rift section *that enlarges at high level to form Gothic Passage which is reached by a climb up a block at waist level 100 m from Waterfall Chamber.* Continuing downstream, the passage becomes more sinuous necessitating occasional traversing in the roof in order to make progress. 1600 m from its start, Southern Stream Passage ends at a junction with Lower Main Stream Passage.

GOTHIC PASSAGE
A climb up from Southern Stream leads to a short traverse into Gothic Passage. A crawl to a T-junction leads to a choice of routes. To the left the passage enlarges for a short distance until another junction is met. *Straight on ends in a dig* while to the right a flat out section and series of uphill squeezes emerges beneath an aven. Skirting the aven, a route through boulders following the wall leads to a hands and knees section of passage through a couple of low crawls into a larger walking sized passage, Priory Road. This continues under a series of avens, *one of which leads into a large high level chamber,* to a low sandy crawl. This emerges in Glevum Hall with a boulder slope up to an area of roof collapse. A series of solution tubes reach a low sandy floored chamber. A further sandy crawl down to the left, leads to another chamber. A squeeze down through boulders at the far end enters a larger chamber containing a massive boulder choke, the Mother of All Battles. A hole on the left hand wall gains entry to a lower series known as The Bunker, and an active dig heading towards the far reaches of Ogof Daren Cilau, less than 30 m away.
Back at the T-junction in Gothic Passage, the right hand route is a low crawl over rocks and up a sandy slope into a large cross passage beneath an aven. *Both left and right eventually close down, but a hole through boulders to the right and across from the point of entry reaches High Traverse Passage. This ends at an 8 m rope climb down into the Lower Main Stream Passage and affords a convenient bypass to the lower end of Southern Stream Passage.* Directly across from the point of entry, Resurrection Passage starts as a low, wide crawl

with occasional enlargements before breaking out into a section of larger passage with a prominent trench in the floor. This enters a series of low sandy crawls to a high aven. The route doubles back through a long excavated section up through a boulder choke. A short section of walking-sized passage follows and leads through a loose boulder choke and down a calcited pile of boulders to an area of fine formations. A further short dig regains a large passage which enters Maytime a little way downstream of Sump 3. Continuing downstream the passage assumes impressive proportions as the water deepens briefly to above the waist. After a small cascade the stream flows through a trench which can be avoided by traversing on wide ledges above the water. A second cascade is then reached, followed by another trench which ends near a small stream inlet on the left. The going becomes easier as the passage goes around several corners before the roof lowers to meet the water at Sump 4.

NORTHERN STREAM PASSAGE
Access to Northern Stream Passage is made through boulders at the start of Southern Stream Passage. A crawl under delicately hung boulders in the floor of the Main Passage leads to a flat out squeeze and a solid roofed passage for 15 m to an aven. The passage then continues for about 150 m passing an area of straws and selenite crystals. A short distance beyond, a crawl over boulders enters a very muddy area and the passage swings to the right leading to a high level and tight tube after a further 120 m. Beyond this the passage continues through a series of low, wet crawls to an area of chokes.

TRIDENT PASSAGE
Trident Passage starts as a high canyon which crosses the stream from the Cliffs of Dover on its way to the 1st Inlet in Southern Stream Passage. A rope climb gains a low crawl which continues for over 600 m of mostly flat out passage interspersed by several small chambers. The passage eventually closes down in an impassable rocky tube with a slight draught and good echo beyond.

ROUND TRIPS
There are a number of popular round trips available in the cave. It is advisable to know both ends of the route before attempting these trips as most of the rescue callouts in the cave are due to parties becoming lost! The round trips are as follows :-**Grand Circle** - Main Passage, Main Stream Passage, Biza Passage, Lower Main Stream Passage, Southern Stream Passage back to Main Passage.
Outer Circle - Turkey Passage, Coal Cellar Passage, Midsummer Passage, Eastern Avenue, Selenite Needle Passage, Sand Caverns Passage back to Turkey Passage.
Inner Circle - Eastern Avenue, Midsummer Passage, Scree Passage, Dome of St.Pauls, Inner Circle Chamber and back to Eastern Avenue.
History   The cave was first explored by SWCC in 1946. Major extensions by HCC in 1957. Grand Circle connected by Eldon Pothole Club in 1972. Remembrance Series and Maytime discovered in 1966-74 by CDG. Further extensions by CSS, SWCC, GSS and others from 1982 onwards. Survey in CSS Records (19) 1992.

Eglwys Faen   Grade 2

Grid Ref SO1928 1568   OS Maps 1:50 000 sheet 161,
1:25 000 Brecon Beacons Eastern O/L

Altitude: 351 metres

Length: 1340 metres

Location   From the CSS hut Whitewalls, follow the old tramroad towards
Agen Allwedd. The tramroad goes around a large bend following the quarries
above, and right in the middle of this bend is a rock spur which juts out to meet
the tramroad from the left. The four entrances to the cave are situated in this
spur.

Description   The cave is mostly dry and presents no real difficulties and is
therefore ideally suited for beginners. The cave is almost certainly associated with
the nearby Agen Allwedd system but as yet no connection has been found.
The largest entrance, which is high up on the right hand side of the spur, leads
directly over boulders into the Main Chamber. The chamber is high and wide for
about 60 m and then the floor rises towards the roof to form a flat-out crawl. The
crawl makes a left turn and then slopes down to a tight squeeze with a strong
draught. Beyond the squeeze the passage becomes larger and leads to another
chamber with a boulder choke at the far end. Entry to an upper series, The
Warren, is gained by climbing up through the boulder choke on the right hand
side. The Warren is a series of small dry passages and tubes negotiated
throughout much of its length by crawling. Digging is still in progress at the
southern end of the Warren but in the other direction a former dig leads to a
streamway and boulder choke. This forms a bypass to Glump Sump in the
Western Series.
In the right hand wall of the Main Chamber near the entrance, an active stream
passage, the Western Series, leads for some distance to reach a concrete dam
with Glump Sump on the left. Going over the concrete dam the passage
continues through a bouldery area to end at a boulder choke.
In the left hand wall of the Main Chamber, a passage connects with the other
entrances. By continuing beyond the chimney entrance to the bottom of a
pothole and turning right, a climb down through a hole in the floor leads to the
Eastern Series and St.Patrick's Passage.

History   The cave has been known for a long time. Survey in CSS Records (19)
1992.

Fell's Swoop   Grade 2
Alternative name: Mud Mine

Grid Ref SO2004 1591   OS Maps 1:50 000 sheet 161,
1:25 000 Brecon Beacons Eastern O/L

Altitude: 345 metres

Length: 91 metres

Location   Follow the old tramroad from Whitewalls towards Agen Allwedd and
Eglwys Faen. At the point where the tramroad suddenly becomes a single track

or path, look back to the left into a small quarry. The entrance is at the far end of the quarry with a walled-up path leading into it.

Description   Most of the cave has been excavated over a period of years to its present length. Progress through most of the cave is by crawling.

The narrow entrance rift leads to a muddy crawl. At the end of this crawl it is possible to stand up in a small chamber. A climb up on the right leads to a short crawl which becomes too tight after about 15 m. Down on the right leads to a short passage ending in a mud choke, while a climb up straight ahead leads to a small passage which ends after about 30 metres or so when it becomes too tight. The last part of this passage contains some small gours.

History   Survey in CSS Records (19) 1992.

Ogof Gwaliau Gwynion   Grade 3
Alternative name: Whitewalls Cave or Channer'sDig

Grid Ref SO2017 1565   OS Maps 1:50 000 sheet 161,
                                            1:25 000 Brecon Beacons Eastern O/L

Altitude: 393 metres

Length: 184 metres

Location   Follow the disused tramroad from the car park past the Daren Cilau quarry until it ends in the Pant-y-Rhiw quarry further around the escarpment. The entrance is situated towards the westerly end of the quarry between two obvious spoil heaps.

Access   The cave is gated and the key is available from the CSS hut Whitewalls.

Description   A crawl zig-zags to the gate. Beyond the passage continues hands and knees sized to a ramp up to a climb into a choke to the right. A crawl enters two well decorated chambers and beyond the passage continues as a flat out crawl to the end of the cave which is close to Puzzle Passage in nearby Ogof Daren Cilau.

History   The first 95 m was almost completely excavated by CSS over several periods from 1970 onwards. Survey in CSS Records (19) 1992.

Ogof Pen Eryr   Grade 3

Grid Ref SO2074 1520   OS Maps 1:50 000 sheet 161,
                                            1:25 000 Brecon Beacons Eastern O/L

Altitude: 408 metres

Length: 426 metres

Location   From the car park 400 m from the CSS hut Whitewalls, follow the path up past disused limekilns to a quarry. Follow this to the left, past the entrance to Ogof Daren Cilau, and just before the end of the quarry the entrance is found at the base of the cliff, about 250 m past Daren Cilau.

Description   This is a good cave for beginners which offers some sporting caving without any serious difficulties or hazards. The cave consists of basically a single passage and therefore provides no navigational problems.

The low entrance leads to a short section of large walking passage and then to a low tight squeeze. Beyond the squeeze it is possible to stand up before reaching a corkscrew squeeze going up at an angle of 45 degrees in the right hand wall. The second part of the corkscrew is tight and not passable to persons of large build. Beyond, a high rift passage leads to a boulder choke. The way on is over the boulders along the left hand wall and then a drop down into the passage below. The passage continues sometimes low, sometimes narrow, to an awkward squeeze over the top of a large boulder with a drop on the other side. After this the passage descends to a low crawl which was originally excavated. At the end of the crawl, a climb up through boulders leads to a more roomy passage stretching in two directions. One way ends after a few metres while the other way continues up and down through the boulder floor for some distance. Near the end a wide low bedding chamber can be entered to the right of the passage and a crawl leads off this to a vandalised grotto. A continuation of the main passage has been excavated and can be followed for about 15 m where it becomes too tight.

History   The cave was first explored by BNSSS in 1959. Survey in CSS Records (19) 1992.

Ogof y Daren Cilau   Grade 5/5+

Grid Ref SO2052 1530   OS Maps 1:50 000 sheet 161,
                                         1:25 000 Brecon Beacons Eastern O/L

Altitude: 399 metres

Length: 26,000 metres approx.

Location   The entrance is situated in the disused quarry behind the car park, 400 m from the CSS hut Whitewalls on the road to Brynmawr. Following the path beside the old limekilns reaches the quarry. The entrance is situated straight ahead, in a small depression below the general ground level, at the base of the cliff.

Description   A very difficult and arduous cave with a long, constricted entrance series leading to extensive passages beyond. The cave deserves its reputation as one of the most serious undertakings in Britain and trips to its further reaches can be extremely demanding in terms of stamina and general physical fitness.

The low entrance leads to a flat-out crawl in the stream and the start of a long constricted passage over 600 m long. A small stream flows along the passage at most times of the year and progress is made by crawling, squeezing, wriggling, and general thrutching for most of its length. 80 m in is a tight squeeze known as The Vice, this is followed by two inlets entering from the right, approximately one third and two thirds of the way through. *The second inlet can be followed to an impenetrable streamway.* The passage briefly enlarges before a series of squeezes between calcited boulders lead to a larger passage at a T-junction. *To the right ends in a choke,* but to the left the way on leads via a short oxbow into a passage littered with boulders. A climb up the boulder slope at the far end emerges in the Old Rift Passage. *To the left the passage quickly ends at a dried up crystal pool. To the right, the rift continues to the Old Main Chamber, Puzzle Passage and the Easter Maze.*

The way on is behind a detached block on the wall opposite from the point of entry. A low crawl leads to a descent through boulders and a short drop down to the top of a calcited boulder slope at the start of Jigsaw Passage. This large muddy passage contains the stream originating in the entrance series and is followed for 300 m to where it appears to close down. A short wriggle through a narrow rift leads to a continuation of the large passage and after another 300 m the passage swings sharp left where an inlet enters from the left. *The inlet, called The Misfit, may be followed for over 400 m to an area of chokes.* A few metres beyond the junction a climb up over boulders enters a large chamber called Big Chamber Nowhere Near The Entrance.

A crawl to the left at the start of the chamber leads to the start of Epocalypse Way, a large and impressive fossil passage which can be followed for several hundred metres passing a fine array of flowstone and helictite formations called the White Company. A little way beyond this, a climb up on a right hand corner leads into Urchin Oxbow which contains some delicate aragonite needles. The main route continues to a point where a small stream crosses the passage at the Kitchen, followed by a climb up a boulder slope. Ahead leads through a crawl into the continuation of the Epocalypse passage and climbs into Locksmith's Passage and the Lower Streamway. Following the left hand wall a crawl enters the start of Antler Passage which contains some large antler-like formations on a bend in the passage a short way along. These are followed by a 6 m climb to where Man In The Roof enters. A ladder ascent beyond this through boulders followed by several climbs and descents through boulders ends in a short section of stream passage and a circular chamber after 600 m. Following a dig through boulders on the right-hand wall gains a further chamber and a boulder run-in on the right. Climbing up through this enters Busman's Holiday which is blocked after a short distance to the right but continues in the opposite direction for 90 m to a low crawl. This leads to a larger passage containing a well decorated chamber and an area of boulder collapse close to the end of The Promised Land in Ogof Craig ar Ffynnon.

To the right in Big Chamber Nowhere Near The Entrance leads to a large scree slope. *Descending the slope enters the Loop Route* but by skirting the wall and ascending the slope to the right reaches the start of Eglwys Passage on the left *and the entrance to Man In The Roof on the right.* Eglwys Passage is followed for about 90 m via a traverse over a hole in the floor and some short crawls to a junction. *Ahead the passage continues to a choke.* Turning left into a small chamber, a well-worn hole in the wall leads into a small pit and a rubble slope to reach the top of St.Valentines Chamber. At the lowest point in the chamber, a hole between boulders leads to a descent of a loose slope into Preliminary Passage and a fixed ladder pitch. At the top of the ladder two routes lead off. *To the right leads to a chamber and boulder choke.* To the left the passage is followed for only a short distance to a small drop and a large hole in the floor. A traverse around the right hand side of the hole gains an ascending slope. At the top of this, a low crawl to the left descends a series of rope climbs down into the large White Passage. *Upstream of the rope climb leads to chokes.*

Downstream, White Passage continues to a pile of boulders and a junction. *To the left is Red River Passage.* Continuing along the main route the passage increases in size until a climb up a huge pile of rocks enters the Time Machine. This is an enormous passage up to 30 m wide. Passing the entrance to Frosty Passage high up on the right hand wall an obvious climb up on the left after 300 m *leads into a high level series.*

THE CAVES OF DAREN CILAU & CRAIG-A-FFYNNON

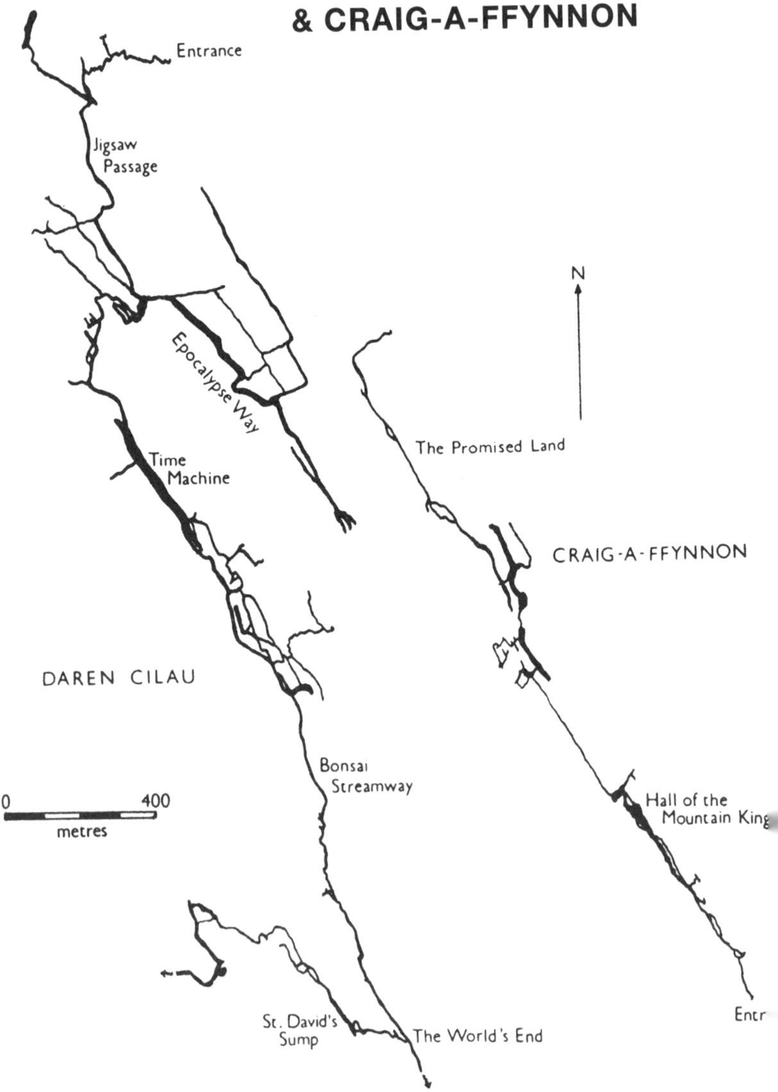

Entrance

Jigsaw Passage

Epocalypse Way

Time Machine

N

The Promised Land

CRAIG-A-FFYNNON

DAREN CILAU

Bonsai Streamway

0   400

metres

Hall of the Mountain King

St. David's Sump

The World's End

Entr

based on surveys by   C.S.S. & G.O.C.A.F.

Continuing along the Time Machine for a further 90 m, several holes to the right drop down into a section of streamway before a boulder choke is encountered. *A route may be forced through the boulders into Beyond Time. A passage to the left enters the Meeting Room or Five Ways Chamber. One route out of the chamber leads back around into the climb down into the Time Machine. In the opposite direction a large passage known as Nameless Canyon passes the entrance to Aggy Passage and Kingston Sands and ends overlooking a drop into Crystal Oxbow. Above the drop a traverse enters Half Mile Passage from which connections with the Western and Eastern Flyovers can be made.* The last of the holes down descends a ramp of sand and boulders into the Bonsai Streamway.

Bonsai Streamway is well decorated in places with straw stalactites and unusual heligmite formations. *A flowstone cascade enters on the left and this is the upstream end of Crystal Oxbow which can be entered from further down the Bonsai Streamway via Crystal Inlet which is also on the left.* Continuing downstream, the passage crosses the start of the Western & Eastern Flyovers at a rockfall before the stream disappears into a narrow rift. A climb up over boulders to the right enters the Kings Road. A little way from the start of this passage, an oxbow to the right leads into the Hard Rock extensions. The main passage ends at a T-junction with a large stream flowing from right to left. Downstream quickly meets the Terminal Sump **WHICH HAS BEEN DIVED FOR 600 M THROUGH TO ELM HOLE IN THE CLYDACH GORGE.** Upstream the passage leads via a swim to St.David's Sump **WHICH IS 40 M LONG.** The upstream side of this sump can be accessed via the Hard Rock Extensions and the Borrowed Boots Streamway.

HARD ROCK EXTENSIONS

The Rock Steady Cruise leads off of the corner in the King's Road oxbow (the site of an underground camp, Hard Rock Cafe). The passage continues through several low sand-filled squeezes enlarging at the end into a low chamber, Brazil. A tight squeeze at the far right hand end of the chamber enters a larger passage *which swings left into the Oregano Trail ending at a large chamber called 12 O'Clock High containing a boulder choke.* Keeping straight on in the large passage, a crawl over a sandbank enters Acupuncture Passage with its sharp rocks and crystals. This eventually enlarges into a sand floored passage with an egg timer like hole in the floor and a rope climb down into an active streamway. *Downstream is the Borrowed Boots Streamway which continues for 300 m passing the start of Saturday Night at the Movies at a 2 m climb. Beyond this a 5 m climb reaches Encillio Passage which lowers to a flat out crawl with a hole in the roof up into further crawling before the passage enters a large oxbow to the main passage of Psychatronic Strangeways. To the right the passage ends at the Gloom Room, a static sump. To the left, a climb up reaches a T-junction with both ways joining an active streamway. Upstream is Duke Sump whilst downstream gains the upstream end of St.David's Sump.*

Upstream from the rope climb, Ankle Grinder Bypass is followed for 500 m over a series of pots in the floor and low sections until it reaches a short duck which can sump in wet weather. Beyond, the passage enlarges and a sand floored passage on the right leads to The Icing on the Cake. Ahead, the streamway ends at 7th Hour Sump **WHICH HAS BEEN DIVED TO A SECOND SUMP AFTER 10 M.** Back from the sump, a 5 m ladder climb enters a large boulder floored chamber, La Plaza, site of a second underground camp known as The Restaurant at the End of the Universe.

A traverse to the left of the ladder leads to a series of well decorated chambers and the start of Pain Killer Passage which ends close to Beyond Time and the end of the Western Flyover. Two passages off to the left unite and encounter a crossroads. Turning left reaches another large chamber and a rift passage with several climbs to a traverse which ends at the head of a 10 m pitch down into Big Chamber (Further From the Entrance Than You Care to Go). At the base of the chamber a large passage, the Inca Trail, heads north through a couple of crawls to a choke. A route to the right gains the continuation of the passage which reaches another choke. Following the left hand wall, the passage swings to the west passing several side passages. Keeping straight on, the passage height lowers to a T-junction. *To the right is a crawl into the Warren.* Keeping to the left, a flat out sandy crawl enters Friday 13th Passage which continues large under a series of avens until pinching out at a boulder choke. A squeeze through a hole to the left enters 100 m of crawling/walking sized passage to Bad Bat Choke. Beyond this the going becomes easier, passing a large side passage which leads to a massive boulder choke before the passage splits and rejoins to end at Spaderunner. *Before this, a small tube in the left hand wall enters Dweebland, a network of passages and chokes close to the end of Priory Road in Agen Allwedd.*

History   The cave was first explored by BNSSS in 1957. Major extensions by CSS in 1984 & 1985, CDG in 1985-87 and others from 1985 onwards. Survey in CSS Records (19) 1992.

WARNING   In very wet weather the whole area around the World's End can sump and back up the King's Road. Also, in very cold weather, the water in the entrance can freeze solid making entry or exit impossible.

Prices Old Dig

Grade 2

Grid Ref SO2106 1492 OS Maps 1:50 000 sheet 161,	
	1:25 000 Brecon Beacons Eastern O/L

Altitude: 410 metres

Length: 95 metres

Location   Follow the old tramroad past the quarry which contains Daren Cilau and Pen Eryr in a southeasterly direction. Several small quarries are passed before reaching a long cliff face. The entrance to the cave is situated at the near end of this quarry, at the base of the cliff.

Description   A short cave which has been partly excavated and is linked hydrologically to Ogof Craig a Ffynnon.

The triangular shaped entrance which is about 1 m wide and 1 m high leads via a short section of damp passage to a climb up through boulders to a low chamber. *To the right is a high aven and also a bedding plane dig*   while to the left a low crawl leads to another chamber. Beyond the second chamber a series of crawls and squeezes lead to a muddy passage which is choked.

History   The cave was first explored and excavated by the CSS. Survey in CSS Records (19) 1992.

Frozen River of Ogof Ffynnon Ddu 2

Neil Weymouth in the phreatic passage, Llygad Llwchwr

Streamway, Ogof Ffynnon Ddu

Pwll y Gwynt

Grade 4

Grid Ref SO1880 1568   OS Maps 1:50 000 sheet 161,
1:25 000 Brecon Beacons Eastern O/L

Altitude: 439 metres

Length: 260 metres approx.
Vertcal Range : 29 metres

Location   The entrance to the cave is a small hole situated 86 m above the tramroad which leads to Agen Allwedd. It is located by ascending the gulley between Eglwys Faen and Aggy, until level with the top of the scree slope on the right. Bear right above the scree until you reach another small gulley. The entrance is situated on the right of this gulley.

Description   A small cave developed along a series of high avens.
A short crawl from the entrance leads to the top of the First Aven and a 21 m pitch. Belay ladder or rope to a scaffold pole which is in situ. Crossing the floor of the aven, a passage is met and the way on is to the left. *To the right leads to a short series of passages under the entrance rift.* To the left a short crawl and a squeeze lead to the Second Aven and then a further short crawl to the Third Aven. The passage enters this aven at a ledge about 5 m above the floor and by following the ledge around you reach another crawl leading to a short climb down into the Fourth Aven.
A crawl at floor level then leads to a cross passage. *To the right becomes too tight after about 10 m* but to the left a climb down and then up leads to a small grotto. Just beyond the grotto the passage continues to a too tight cross passage but before this a low crawl on the left leads to a much larger passage ending in a crawl back to the foot of the Third Aven. About 10 m along the large passage, a rift in the roof gives access to the Fifth Aven. The way on is up, via a 10 m rope climb. At the top bear around to the right in small passages to the Sixth Aven and a 6 m ladder pitch (bolt in place). A way on from the aven can be followed to a slot in the floor and a short drop into a small stream. This can be followed via a small chamber until it becomes too tight after about 20 m or so.

Tackle   First Aven - 25 m rope or ladder and lifeline
Fifth Aven - 10 m ladder and lifeline (first man up needs prussiking gear)
Sixth Aven - 6 m ladder and lifeline

History   Discovered by CSS in 1981. Survey in CSS Records (19) 1992.

Pwll y Pasg

Grade 3

Grid Ref SO1822 1607   OS Maps 1:50 000 sheet 161,
1:25 000 Brecon Beacons Eastern O/L

Altitude: 479 metres

Length: 355 metres

Location   The entrance is situated in a shakehole on the moor above Agen Allwedd and is difficult to find. Follow the track past Aggy and climb up the gully which goes between the cliff faces. Once on the top, head over to your right to an area of shakeholes. The entrance is in one of these shakeholes and is sometimes marked by a cairn.

Description   The cave is a typical shakehole cave developed just below the surface of the moor.

The entrance crawl leads to a small chamber from which a further crawl leads above a hole in the floor to a junction. To the left a muddy passage continues for some distance before closing down. To the right leads via some short crawls to a 15 m blind shaft. More crawling leads to another shaft, 17 m deep, with loose boulders at the top. At the bottom of this shaft a very narrow rift passage ends in loose boulders. Both shafts are rather unpleasant with constrictions and razor sharp rock.

A recent extension connects with the neighbouring Ogof Llungwyn.

Tackle   1st Shaft - 15 m ladder and lifeline (belay to iron bar)
            2nd Shaft - 17 m ladder and lifeline + short belay

History   First recorded exploration was by the TSU. Extended in 1992 by CSS. Survey in CSS Records (19) 1992.

Lesser Caves and Sites of Speleological Interest

Ap Derek   SO2145 1465
Capel Faen   SO1935 1565
Cwm Pant Lladron (doline)   SO1651 1625
Fox Holes   SO2085 1515
Ivy Rift   SO1982 1584
Llangattwg Swallet   SO1930 1540
Moult's Hole   SO1918 1561
Mud Cave   SO2100 1500
Ogof a'r Olygfa Braf   SO1991 1582
Ogof Bannau   SO1880 1567
Ogof Bos Lethri   SO1876 1587
Ogof Ffu   SO1855 1619
Ogof Grug Hywel   SO1977 1538
Ogof Llungwyn   SO1823 1606
Ogof Newport   SO1823 1611
Ogof Pen y Gwent   SO1989 1583
Ogof Tynol y Gareg   SO1873 1567
Pastie Digs   SO2095 1510
Prices New Dig   SO2080 1517
Pwll Estrys   SO1924 1545
Rowan Pot Dig   SO1614 1654
Twll y Cadno   SO2035 1510
Twll y Llwynog   SO1875 1588
Waen Rudd (doline)   SO1837 1566

4. Central Northern Outcrop

Blaen Onneu Quarry Pot
Alternative name : Pwll Blaen Onneu

Grade 3/4

Grid Ref SO1589 1620   OS Maps 1:50000 sheet 161,
1:25000 Brecon Beacons Eastern O/L

Altitude : 498 metres

Length : 426 metres
Depth : 74 metres

Location   Turn north from the Heads of the Valleys Road at Beaufort onto the B4560 towards Llangynidr. After a little over 3 km the road starts to descend and a rough track on the left leads to the old Blaen Onneu quarry (marked on OS maps). The entrance is situated in the quarry floor under a boulder.
Access   A gate has been installed in the passage leading to the southern extensions. For details of access contact A.Dickenson on 0452 770310.
Description   The entrance is small hole in the quarry floor opening out into the passage below. The pitch is about 3.6 m deep and can be descended with the help of a ladder or rope. The passage entered is a high rift and can be followed to the north and to the south.
To the north, the passage soon reaches a narrow pitch. Belay ladder or rope to an iron bar wedged between the walls. At the bottom of the pitch a rift passage leads to a shattered area and then to a smaller passage with several squeezes leading to a chamber. *A small passage to the right leads to a narrow meander which lowers to a crawl and ends at a choke.* On the other side of the chamber is a large boulder choke, this can be passed on the left to a space above the choke and a 2.2 m pitch into another chamber. On the far side a crawl leads to another chamber.
To the south, from below the entrance pitch, the high rift descends over boulders before the roof lowers at a shattered area. An excavated crawl beyond the gate then leads to the Twin Peaks, a 9 m pitch. *Two small passages lead northwest and southeast from the bottom of the pitch but both end within a short distance.* The way on is via an excavated hole in a small chamber to the north of Twin peaks. This leads to a tight crawl and a 5 m pitch into a chamber. From here a passage runs southeast and a small stream is met before the passage closes down.
Tackle   Entrance Pitch - 4 m ladder or rope, belay and lifeline
1st Northern Pitch - 11 m ladder, belay and lifeline
2nd Northern Pitch - 3 m ladder, belay and lifeline
Twin Peaks Pitch - 10 m ladder or rope, belay & lifeline
Final Pitch - 5 m ladder, bealy and lifeline
History   First explored by SWCC in 1948. Extended by Llanelly Diggers in 1990 & 1991. Survey Llanelly Diggers 1992.

58

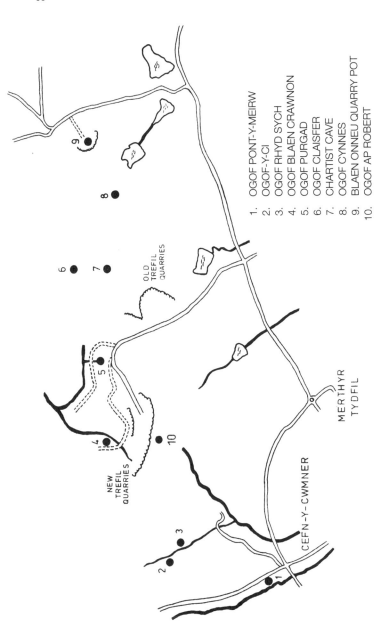

1. OGOF PONT-Y-MEIRW
2. OGOF-Y-CI
3. OGOF RHYD SYCH
4. OGOF BLAEN CRAWNON
5. OGOF PURGAD
6. OGOF CLAISFER
7. CHARTIST CAVE
8. OGOF CYNNES
9. BLAEN ONNEU QUARRY POT
10. OGOF AP ROBERT

OLD TREFIL QUARRIES

NEW TREFIL QUARRIES

MERTHYR TYDFIL

CEFN-Y-CWMNER

CENTRAL NORTHERN OUTCROP

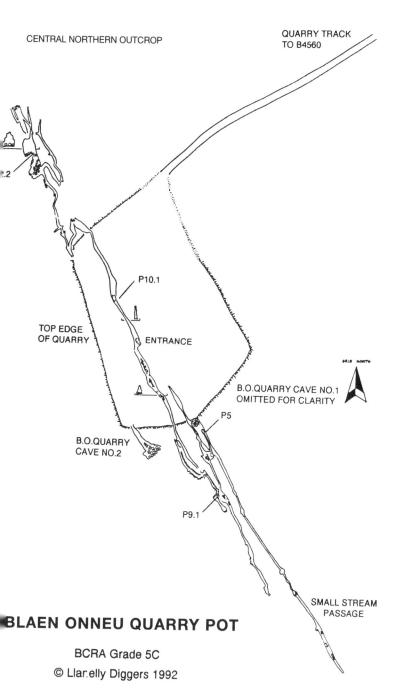

CENTRAL NORTHERN OUTCROP

QUARRY TRACK
TO B4560

P10.1

ENTRANCE

TOP EDGE
OF QUARRY

B.O.QUARRY CAVE NO.1
OMITTED FOR CLARITY

P5

B.O.QUARRY
CAVE NO.2

P9.1

SMALL STREAM
PASSAGE

BLAEN ONNEU QUARRY POT

BCRA Grade 5C

© Llanelly Diggers 1992

Chartists Cave

Grid Ref SO1280 1520   OS Maps 1:50000 sheet 161,
1:25000 Brecon Beacons Central O/L

Altitude : 533 metres

Length : 400 metres approx.

Location   A difficult cave to find. From the Heads of the Valleys Road take the small side road leading to the village of Trefil. Just beyond the village there are some extensive quarry workings on the right. Climb up onto the top of the moor behind the quarries and head for the summit of Mynydd Llangynidr. The entrance to the cave is near the summit in a small rock outcrop and is marked on OS maps but is easily overlooked.

Description   A small but interesting cave beyond which there must be considerable passage still to be discovered.

A broad entrance arch gives access to a chamber from which there are two ways on. *The passage to the right is initially low but then rises and opens out before ending after about 30 m.* To the left, the passage leads after a short distance to a small hole below loose debris. Beyond is a high rift passage about 6 m long. *A high level continuation goes straight ahead but soon becomes too tight.* The way on is at floor level to the left, down over boulders to a short crawl. The crawl leads to a complex of very large sandy passages and narrow meandering rifts. There is no obvious way on.

History   The first part of the cave has been known for a very long time and there are many stories relating to it. Extended by SVCC in 1969.

Ogof Ap Robert

Grid Ref SO0990 1340   OS Maps 1:50000 sheet 161,
1:25000 Brecon Beacons Central O/L

Length : 1015 metres
Depth : 90 metres

Location   Situated on the mountain behind the working quarry near Trefil and is difficult to find. Follow the road through Trefil and about 400 m before reaching the quarry there is a path on the left which leads up onto the mountain. The entrance to the cave is a swallet which takes water at the base of a 10 m high cliff face about 2 km to 2.5 km from the start of the path.

Description   An active swallet whose water resurges at the Sion-Sieffri Reservoir to the south of Trefil village. This is approximately 3 km distant and 150 m lower than the terminal boulder choke in the cave.

The cave descends steeply via a series of narrow rifts and intersecting small passages, many of which are filled with surface debris and boulder chokes. The First Boulder Choke is supported by scaffolding and shoring, and great care must be taken when going through it. After the 1st BC, the cave continues to descend steeply via rifts and vertical drops, all of which can be free-climbed. This gives access via another small section of boulder choke which is supported by scaffolding, to a large collapsed chamber called Toad Hall. Several short interconnecting passages lead off from this chamber including a significant inlet

"Twyn Ceiliog "which is to the right of the chamber and can be climbed upwards for about 30 m in major aven development.

The main way on is via a hole in the floor through boulders on the left-hand side of Toad Hall. The first 30 m is under the floor of the chamber and is extremely unstable and should not be undertaken when there is heavy rain outside. This gives access to a series of dry phreatic passages, the water disappearing down a rift in the floor. By turning right at a junction, South Passage can be followed for some 150 m with various inlets being encountered on the way. By turning left at the junction and then bearing left, access is gained to North Passage which passes alongside and below Toad Hall until the passage becomes too tight to follow after approx. 150 m. The main way on is by turning left at the junction and then bearing right to a ladder pitch through boulders. At the bottom the stream is regained and enters the present final choke which can be descended for about 10 m without finding an obvious way on. The whole boulder choke area is extremely unstable.

Tackle   Boulder Pitch - 8 m ladder, belay and lifeline

History   The swallet has been dug by various groups over a number of years but without any great success. The most recent efforts by GOCAF and GSS led to the major discoveries after intensive digging in 1987.

Ogof Blaen Crawnon   Grade 3

Grid Ref SO0950 1494 OS Maps 1:50000 sheet 161,	
	1:25000 Brecon Beacons Central O/L

Altitude : 442 metres

Length : 91 metres

Location   Follow the road from Trefil, past the old quarries, to where two large boulders on the right mark the track which leads down into Cwm Purgad. Just past this track, another track also on the right, which is an old quarry tramroad, runs along the top of Cwm Purgad and then beneath the new Trefil quarries. Follow the track to the point where a large stream crosses under it and drops in a waterfall to the valley below. The entrance to the cave is a few metres past the waterfall at the base of a small cliff. A small stream issues from the cave.

Description   A small immature stream cave which is the resurgence for water sinking at a small cave called Ogof Waen Rydd situated about 1200 m to the west. The low entrance leads to a narrow streamway. The stream is followed upstream along a tight and narrow passage to where the water issues from a sump pool on the left. This is bypassed by a passage on the right which then bears around to the left and back into the stream. More squeezing and crawling leads to some deep pools and then the passage turns sharp left. The passage becomes progressively smaller and eventually ends at another sump. **THIS SUMP HAS BEEN DIVED FOR 11 M VIA SEVERAL TIGHT BENDS AND THE PASSAGE CAN BE SEEN TO CONTINUE.** There are also two small side passages, one of which can be followed for some distance.

History   The cave was first explored by BNSSS in 1959.

Ogof Claisfer

Grade 2

Grid Ref SO1290 1610   OS Maps 1:50000 sheet 161,
1:25000 Brecon Beacons Central O/L

Altitude : 488 metres

Length : 60 metres approx.

Location   To the northeast of Mynydd Llangynidr and Chartists Cave is a deep valley containing the Claisfer Resurgence. On the northern side of the valley, not far from the resurgence, are some small but obvious rock outcrops. The entrance to the cave is in the most westerly outcrop.

Description   A small dry cave probably associated with the nearby resurgence. The entrance is a short pot at the foot of the outcrop. At the bottom of the pot a crawl leads to a small chamber. From here a descending crawl to the right leads to another small chamber below the first. By climbing up to the right part way down the descending crawl a narrow rift is gained. Beyond this is a maze of interconnecting narrow passages which all become too tight or choked with mud and stones.

History   The cave was first explored and surveyed by BNSSS in 1959.

Ogof Cynnes

Grade 4

Grid Ref SO1408 1540   OS Maps 1:50000 sheet 161,
1:25000 Brecon Beacons Central O/L

Altitude : 524 metres

Length : 1200 metres approx.

Location   Situated on the moor and is difficult to find. It is best approached from the Blaen Onneu Quarry (see Blaen Onneu Quarry Pot). Head roughly west towards the trig point and then from there turn slightly south of west for about 800 metres to the head of a large dry valley. There is a small rock outcrop and a cairn on this side of the valley with two oblong shaped shakeholes nearby. The larger of the shakeholes looks like a miniature sunken gorge and the entrance to the cave is in the uphill side of the shakehole.

Description   An interesting and very sporty cave which is dry but exceedingly muddy. Parts of the cave are difficult and very arduous and should therefore only be attempted by fit or experienced cavers.

The entrance slot, which is in millstone grit, drops down into a small chamber. A further short drop over boulders leads to a large blind pot on the right. Straight ahead a narrow rift leads after a few metres to a tight awkward squeeze on the right. The squeeze leads to a tight sloping passage and a pitch. Belay ladder to an iron bar wedged above the squeeze (a ladder is recommended as muddy hands on the return journey make the ascent by rope rather precarious). At the bottom of the pitch a climb up into a narrow rift and crawl leads to a fixed rope. The rope drops into a narrow muddy slot, the ascent of which can prove very difficult on the return journey. At the bottom of the slot a low arch in deep glutenous mud leads to a larger passage. *To the left several passages go for a short distance* but the way on is to the right. The right-hand passage soon becomes blocked by boulders but a way through can be found on the right and this leads to a fixed ladder which drops into the large Main Chamber, some 10-12 m high. At the far end of the chamber two passages lead off. The passage on the right leads to a very extensive and complex series of muddy crawls and passages running parallel with the entrance series and leading to the Easter Series. This series comprising of bedding planes, rifts and some small chambers ends at a too tight bedding plane beyond a sizeable chamber.

To the left of the Main Chamber a high rift passage leads to more muddy passages and crawls.

There is a strong draught throughout much of the cave.

Tackle   First Pitch - 8 m ladder, belay and lifeline
            Muddy Slot - a clean 4 m rope is useful

History   The cave was first explored by HCC in 1967. Easter Series discovered in 1993. Survey M.Farr & I.Homes 1969. Easter Series, B.Lovett et al 1993, Descent (112).

Ogof Pont-y-Meirw   Grade 3

Grid Ref SO0250 0840   OS Maps 1:50000 sheet 160,
                                        1:25000 Brecon Beacons Central O/L

Altitude : 240 metres

Length : 112 metres

Location   Situated in the south bank of the Taf Fawr near Cefn Coed cemetery. The entrance is about 50 metres upstream from a bridge connecting the two halves of the cemetery.

Description   Only the first 36 m of the cave is accessible to non-divers. The entrance passage ends in a sump which **HAS BEEN PASSED BY DIVERS FOR A DISTANCE OF ABOUT 76 M.**

History   The cave was first explored by I.C.I.Fibres S.S. in 1964.

Ogof Purgad   Grade 3

Grid Ref SO1046 1536   OS Maps 1:50000 sheet 161,
                                        1:25000 Brecon Beacons Central O/L

Altitude : 396 metres

Length : 122 metres

Location   Follow the road from Trefil past the old quarries to where two large boulders on the right mark the track which leads down into Cwm Purgad. Follow the track into the Cwm until a stream cascades down on the left to flow under the track. Climb up the cascade to where the stream issues from the base of a small cliff. The entrance to the cave is behind a shower coming from a higher level stream.

Description   A small but sporty cave with much sharp rock. Progress through the cave is mostly by crawling.

The entrance leads to a narrow rift. After a short distance, a passage on the left leads to a sporty crawl in water. This passage ends after about 45 m when it becomes too tight. Straight on from the entrance rift the passage becomes much narrower and a tight squeeze through leads to a junction. Water issues from an impenetrable passage on the right while to the left a crawl leads for about 60 m over sharp rock until it becomes too tight.

History   The cave was first explored by SWCC.

Ogof Rhyd Sych

Grade 4

Grid Ref SO0412 1021	OS Maps 1:50000 sheet 160,
	1:25000 Brecon Beacons Central O/L

Altitude : 292 metres

Length : 1097 metres

Location   At Cefn Coed the A470 Merthyr to Brecon road crosses a bridge over the Heads of the Valleys Road (A465). Turn immediately right after the bridge, towards Pontsticill, and follow the road for about 2.5 km to the point where the road bends sharply to the right over a stone bridge which spans the Nant-y-Glais stream. Continue up the road to the Pont Sarn Hotel where cars can be parked. A footpath opposite the hotel leads back to the Nant-y-Glais valley. On reaching a small gorge a stream can be seen issuing from the cave in the left bank.

Description   A large and interesting cave with some tight, wet, and sporting sections at the beginning and ending in some very large passages. One section of the bedding plane is very tight and is not passable to persons of larger than average build.

The entrance gives access to a short section of lofty stream passage leading to a duck. The way on is through the duck and into a small chamber and then down a small hole on the far side. A short crawl leads to another hole into deep water. *Beyond the water the passage continues straight ahead* but the way on is via a low mud crawl on the right which leads to a bedding plane chamber. Turn left and then right across the bedding plane which slopes at a 45 degree angle. Squeeze down over boulders into a continuation of the bedding plane, at the far side of which the stream can be heard through a very low section of continuing bedding plane. The way on is through this low section and is very tight. Progress is made by inching forward slowly and picking a route which is large enough to allow the body through. *There is an alternative high level route but it is much longer, also very tight in places and the way back into the streamway is complicated.* Once into the stream it is followed upstream until it becomes possible to walk upright for a short distance in a narrow streamway. A climb up then leads to a further section of wet bedding plane crawl.

The floor of the bedding plane has been carved out by the stream and is rather uncomfortable but it eventually opens up and the first calcite formations are encountered. A drop down a hole in the floor leads back into the stream and after a short crawl a stream chamber is entered with some fine formations. At the far end of the chamber a climb over calcite gives access to a very large passage and a complete change in the character of the cave. A huge boulder slope rises on the left and the way on is over the top on the right-hand side. Continue over the boulders and then drop down on the right into a short section of streamway. A climb up on the left then leads to a passage and a vertical drop which can be descended without gear by sticking closely to the right-hand wall. At the bottom, the stream runs in a huge chamber which is blocked at the far end by a large boulder choke. A passage has been made through the boulders low down on the left but it is very loose and ends in a jumble of small boulders.

Tackle   A wetsuit is advisable.
History   First explored by the SWCC in 1950. Extended by BNSSS in 1957.
Major extensions made by CCC in 1967.
WARNING : THE CAVE IS LIABLE TO FLOOD. The duck just inside the cave can
sump. In severe flood the water backs up within the cave to a considerable height.

Ogof Robin Goch
Grade 2

Grid Ref SO0392 1075   OS Maps 1:50000 sheet 160,
1:25000 Brecon Beacons Central O/L

Altitude : 312 metres

Length : 130 metres

Location   Situated about 50 m below Blaen y Glais Farm in the Nant-y-Glais
Valley. The entrance is a hole in the east bank which takes flood water from the
Nant-y-Glais stream.
Description   The small entrance passage is followed to a T-junction with a wide
bedding plane passage. *To the left quickly becomes too tight* but to the right
the passage continues low and becomes even lower before entering a large
chamber with a boulder choke at the far end. This choke is thought to be directly
associated with the choke at the furthest point reached in Ogof Rhyd Sych.
There is a side passage to the right of the chamber but all ways end too tight.
History   Surveyed by ICC.
WARNING :   THE CAVE IS LIABLE TO FLOOD.

Ogof-y-Ci
Grade 2

Grid Ref SO0404 1047   OS Maps 1:50000 sheet 160,
1:25000 Brecon Beacons Central O/L

Length : 548 metres

Location   The cave is situated on the left-hand side of the Nant-y-Glais stream a
few hundred metres upstream from Ogof Rhyd Sych. A stream resurges from the
lower entrance while just above it there is a dry entrance which is the more
normal route. There is a third entrance about 150 metres further upstream.
The cave should be approached from Llwyn-y-Ci Farm (park cars by the remains
of an old barn on the lane leading to the farm). Consult the farmer as he
sometimes keeps a bull in the field to be crossed. Go through the farmyard and
turn right through a gate. Turn immediately left and follow the fence to a stile into
the gorge. The entrance to the cave is a few metres upstream.
Description   A good cave for beginners giving them a taste of an active stream
cave without involving them in any real dangers. The cave consists of a single
main streamway, taking water from the Nant-y-Glais stream, with several small
dry side passages all of which end after a short distance.
The lower entrances lead into an active stream passage most of which is crawling
for the first 60 m. The passage then becomes much larger and after some
distance daylight can be seen coming from the third entrance on the right. Soon
after the third entrance is passed the roof lowers dramatically but the passage
continues for some considerable way becoming progressively smaller.
Tackle   A wetsuit is an advantage but not essential.

Taf Fawr Caves

Grade 3

Grid Ref SO0270 0810   OS Maps 1:50000 sheet 160,
1:25000 Brecon Beacons Central O/L

Altitude : 195 metres

Length : 186 metres

Location   Situated on the right bank of the Taf Fawr at Cefn Coed-y-Cymmer, a little over 3 km north of Merthyr Tydfil.
Description   There are two small caves of little interest to ordinary cavers. **HOWEVER, ONE OF THE CAVES CONNECTS WITH THE NEARBY PWLL TAF RESURGENCE VIA A 118 M SUMP CALLED THE FOREST TRAIL.**

Lesser Caves and Sites of Speleological Interest

Badger Den   SO0980 1510
Balcony Cave   SO1230 1340
Baltic Quarry Cave   SO0640 1160
Blaen Onneu Quarry Caves   SO1583 1623
Blaen Rhymney Resurgence   SO0995 1082
Cefn Coed Risings   SO0305 0775
Claisfer Resurgence   SO1290 1601
Crescent Cave   SO1290 1510
Cwar yr Ystrad Caves   SO0880 1450
Dereks Dig   SO1000 1370
Dolygaer Station Cave   SO0575 1450
Ffynnon Cae Rhos   SO1368 1608
Ffynnon Shon Sheffrey   SO1265 1188
Lake Sink   SO1100 1300
Mantles Hole   SO1510 1680
Morlais Castle Resurgence   SO0480 0990
North Rift   SO1200 1380
Odyn Fach Sink   SO0890 1250
Ogof Cneuen   SO0395 1077
Ogof Ebill   SO1070 1440
Ogof Fach Trefil   SO0940 1460
Ogof Garn Galch   SO1460 1660
Ogof Hen Gwar Trefil   SO1220 1360
Ogof Johnny Bach   SO0424 1001
Ogof Llwynog   SO1002 1518
Ogof Mynydd Llangynidr   SO1540 1580
Ogof Taf Fechan   SO0480 1010
Ogof y Carreg Wen   SO1460 1650
Ogof y Cornel   SO0660 1020
Pontsticil Resurgence   SO0620 1050
Pwll Coch   SO1655 1508
Pwll y Gaer   SO0610 1488
Tyle Haidd Quarry Resurgence   SO0630 1050
Vaynor Church Risings   SO0490 1020

5. Sychryd Gorge & Hepste Valley Area

Blaen Hepste Resurgence

Grid Ref SN9614 1279   OS Maps 1:50000 sheet 160,
1:25000 Brecon Beacons Central O/L

Length : 268 metres

Location   Situated in the upper part of the Hepste Valley.
Description   A resurgence only accessible to divers.
TWO ROUTES, SUMP 1 AND SUMP 1A, LEAD AFTER 30 M TO A LARGE AIRBELL AT THE
START OF SUMP 2. SUMP 2 IS 190 M LONG AND STARTS AS A VERTICAL DROP DOWN A
RIFT OF 8 M INTO A LARGER PASSAGE WHICH IS FOLLOWED THROUGH A SERIES OF
DROPS TO A DEPTH OF 10-11 M. AT THE END, A VERTICAL SQUEEZE THROUGH A
BOULDER CHOKE LEADS TO AN AIRBELL WITH A SADDLE OF ROCK. SUMP 3 STARTS
AS A POT ON THE OTHER SIDE OF THE SADDLE AND IS 38 M LONG WITH A MAXIMUM
DEPTH OF 11 M PASSING A CHOKE ON THE WAY TO A SMALL AIRBELL. SUMP 4
STARTS FROM THIS AIRBELL AND HAS BEEN DIVED FOR 10 M.
History   Explored by the CDG since 1965. Survey 1991, Descent (99).

Moss Risings   Grade 2
Alternative name : Ogof Abercwrier

Grid Ref SN9698 1328   OS Maps 1:50000 sheet 160,
1:25000 Brecon Beacons Central O/L

Altitude : 328 metres

Length : 260 metres approx.

Location   Situated in the upper part of the Hepste Valley about 800 m upstream
from Blaen Hepste. There is a large rising near to a Water Works building. The
entrance to the cave is at the back of the depression containing the rising.
Description   Although the cave is basically a divers cave, the first 60 m or so is
accessible to non-divers in normal weather conditions.
The narrow entrance turns immediately sharp left in water to a wide chamber. A
climb over the mud bank straight ahead leads into a continuation of the chamber
ending in deep water and a sump. To the left of the mud bank, a crawl leads
through several right-angled bends to a waterworn passage which ends after
about 27 m in a sump. THIS SUMP HAS BEEN DIVED FOR A DISTANCE OF
APPROXIMATELY 200 M.
Tackle   A wet suit is advisable.
History   Explored by the CDG.
WARNING : THE CAVE IS LIABLE TO FLOOD.

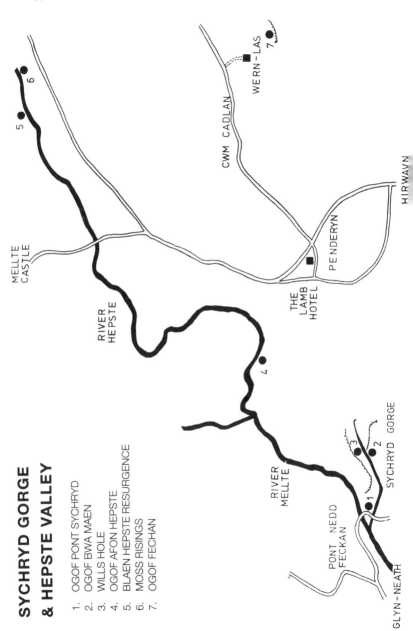

SYCHRYD GORGE
& HEPSTE VALLEY

1. OGOF PONT SYCHRYD
2. OGOF BWA MAEN
3. WILLS HOLE
4. OGOF AFON HEPSTE
5. BLAEN HEPSTE RESURGENCE
6. MOSS RISINGS
7. OGOF FECHAN

Ogof Afon Hepste

Grade 3

Grid Ref SN9383 0968   OS Maps 1:50000 sheet 160,
1:25000 Brecon Beacons Central O/L

Altitude : 234 metres

Length : 1400 metres approx.

Location   Situated at the lower end of the Hepste Valley. Access should be made via the path from Penderyn and not along the Hepste dry valley. The entrance is a small hole in the bank of the dry river bed about 50 metres downstream from a fallen tree.

Description   A major cave system which is basically only accessible to divers. However, in very dry weather the first 244 m can be explored by non-divers. A careful watch must be kept on the weather as the cave floods with alarming ease. The entrance leads to a small descending passage and then a short drop into Pipe Passage. This leads to Sump 1 which in dry weather becomes a small pool. *Beyond and to the left leads to the Western Streamway and the sumps into Ogof Tarddiant Hepste and Ogof Tram Trucks further downstream. There are bypasses to the first two sumps but the way on into O.T.H. is only passable by divers.*

To the right after Sump 1 leads to Sump 2 which is only passable by divers. ABOUT 30 M BEYOND THE END OF SUMP 2 THE PASSAGE CAN BE FOLLOWED TO THE LEFT OR RIGHT. TO THE LEFT IS THE MAIN STREAMWAY AND TO THE RIGHT IS THE EASTERN PASSAGE. THE MAIN STREAMWAY CONTINUES TO SUMP 3 WHICH IS 152 M LONG LEADING TO 20 M OF PASSAGE. SUMP 4 CAN BE BYPASSED BY A HIGH LEVEL PASSAGE TO A SMALL PIT. 30 M BEYOND THIS IS SUMP 5 WHICH IS 22 M LONG FOLLOWED BY A SERIES OF PASSAGES WHICH END WITHIN A SHORT DISTANCE OF THE HEPSTE RIVER AT A POINT 130 M SOUTH OF THE FORD AT BRYN CUL.

THE EASTERN PASSAGE STARTS AS A LOW MUDDY CRAWL TO SUMP 1 WHICH IS 20 M LONG LEADING TO A CANAL. THERE IS ALSO A DRY BYPASS TO THE LEFT OF THE SUMP WHICH ALSO LEADS TO THE CANAL. BEFORE REACHING SUMP 2, THE WORM RIFT IS ENTERED TO THE RIGHT AND THIS BYPASSES BOTH SUMP 2 AND SUMP 3. SUMP 4 IS 9 M LONG FOLLOWED BY 61 M OF PASSAGE TO SUMP 5 WHICH IS 24 M LONG. 18 M OF PASSAGE THEN LEADS TO SUMP 6 WHICH IS 20 M LONG FOLLOWED BY 114 M OF PASSAGE TO SUMP 7. THIS IS 12 M LONG AND IS FOLLOWED IMMEDIATELY BY SUMP 8 WHICH BECOMES CHOKED AFTER A FURTHER 12 M.

History   Ogof Tarddiant Hepste is an obvious cave under a waterfall and has been known for a long time. Ogof Afon Hepste entrance was discovered by WSG in 1968 and has been further extended since that time by the CDG.

Survey   1979, UBSS Proceedings 15 (2).

WARNING : THE CAVE IS LIABLE TO SEVERE FLOODING.

Ogof Bwa Maen

Grade 1

Alternative name : Fireplace Hole

Grid Ref SN9160 0804   OS Maps 1:50000 sheet 160,
1:25000 Brecon Beacons Central O/L

Altitude : 93 metres

Length : 91 metres

Location   The cave is situated in the Sychryd Gorge. From Glyn Neath follow the road to Pont Nedd Fechan and then take the right-hand fork towards Craig-y-Dinas and the Sychryd Gorge. A wide track leads up through the gorge to the remains of a ramp which leads up to the old silica mines. Across the river from the foot of the ramp is the large cavernous opening of Bwa Maen.

Description   The large entrance chamber is entered by crossing the river. A climb up on the right-hand side of the entrance can be tackled via several routes all of which converge high up in the chamber. A further short climb to the roof leads to a small passage. By bearing left it is possible to overlook the entrance chamber while to the right a waterworn passage runs parallel to the gorge outside. A climb down one or two short drops then leads to a small chamber. From here, a low crawl in water leads to another small chamber with several ways off which all become too tight after a short distance.

History   The cave was first explored by SWCC in 1951.

Ogof Fechan

Grade 4

Alternative name : Ogof Fach

Grid Ref SN9707 0972   OS Maps 1:50000 sheet 160,
1:25000 Brecon Beacons Central O/L

Altitude : 297 metres

Length : 1067 metres

Location   From Penderyn take the turning opposite the Lamb Hotel towards Cwm Cadlan. Follow the road along the Cwm until it reaches the farm of Wernlas. A track leads past the farm, crosses a stream and then peters out. Head across the field towards a gate in a stone wall. Beyond the gate bear right and descend to the floor of the valley where a stream sinks at the base of a small rock outcrop. The entrance to the cave is below corrugated sheets near the top of the outcrop.

Access   Permission to visit the cave should be obtained from Wernlas farm.

Description   An interesting and sporting cave, most of which is active streamway with very few side passages.

The muddy entrance shaft leads to a small chamber. The stream can be heard to the left but the way on is to the right through boulders in the floor to a narrow rift. A climb down the rift leads to a crawl which in turn leads to the streamway. A section of fine streamway then follows until the water disappears on the right. A low crawl straight ahead leads into Sand Chamber.. Bearing left across the chamber, *Inlet Stream Passage comes in from the left* while under the right-hand wall a hole leads down through boulders to the stream. After a very short distance the water disappears again and a distinctive crawl developed in a shale band is followed to

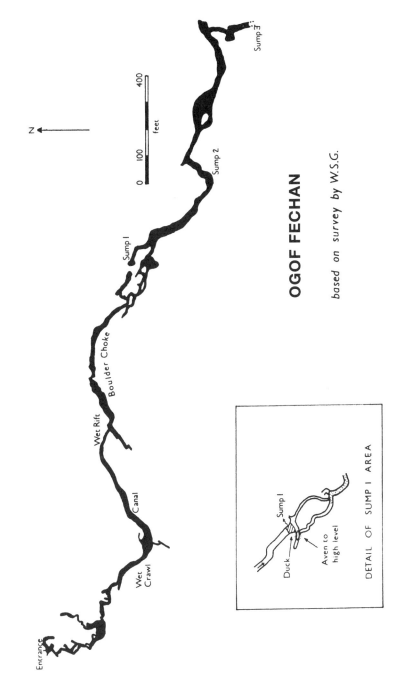

OGOF FECHAN

based on survey by W.S.G.

N

feet
0   100   400

Entrance

Wet Crawl

Canal

Wet Rift

Boulder Choke

Sump 1

Sump 2

Sump 3

DETAIL OF SUMP 1 AREA

Sump 1

Duck

Aven to high level

the right. The crawl rejoins the streamway after about 10 m at the bottom of a steep water chute. Downstream, a low section of passage is followed to a small waterfall into a chamber. Beyond the chamber is the Wet Crawl or First Canal. This is a hands and knees crawl in water leading to a large chamber with a high mud bank on the left-hand wall. The stream flows through the chamber which gradually loses height to the start of the Canal, this being another hands and knees crawl in water but this time much longer, about 45 m. At the end of the Canal, the water again disappears to the right but straight ahead is the West Rift, a narrow passage with some fine calcite formations and deep water at the end leading back into the streamway. Downstream the passage soon becomes blocked by a large boulder choke which is passed by going to the top of the choke and then up through a small hole into an aven. The way on then leads to another aven and then much crawling and scrambling over and under boulders follows. The route gradually works its way back to the stream and then to Sump 1.

Sump 1 goes off to the left of the sump pool but it can be bypassed via a duck straight ahead. There is a line running through the duck to a narrow cross passage on the other side. A short distance to the right beyond the duck there is a tight awkward climb up which emerges in the floor of a high level passage. In one direction the passage ends after a very short distance while in the other direction it leads for about 55 m to Waterfall Chamber. By crossing the chamber and following the left-hand wall leads to the large an impressive streamway. *Upstream after about 30 m is the downstream end of Sump 1* while downstream the passage gradually becomes lower to end at Sump 2 after about 76 m.

SUMP 2 IS ONLY PASSABLE TO DIVERS AND IS 15 M LONG TO AN AIRBELL FOLLOWED BY A FURTHER 12 M. AN OPEN STREAMWAY OF 260 M THEN LEADS TO SUMP 3. THIS IS A DIVE OF 15 M TO AN AIRBELL FOLLOWED BY A FURTHER 54 M TO A CROSS PASSAGE, BEYOND WHICH THE PASSAGE QUICKLY BECOMES TOO CONSTRICTED FOR FURTHER PROGRESS.

Tackle   A wet suit is essential.

History   First explored by Monmouth School C.C. in the 1950's. Extended by OUCC in 1965. Major extentions made by WSG in 1970.

Survey   WSG Bulletin 7 (7).

WARNING : THE CAVE IS LIABLE TO FLOOD.

Ogof Glan Hepste/Tucks Rift

Grid Ref SN9519 1182 (Glan Hepste) SN9518 1185 (Tucks Rift)
            OS Maps 1:50000 sheet 160, 1:25000 Brecon Beacons Central O/L

Altitude : 291 metres

Length : 500 metres approx.

Location   Situated in the middle part of the Hepste Valley about 1.6 km downstream from Blaen Hepste.

Description   A divers cave with very little dry passage.

THERE ARE TWO ENTRANCES TO GLAN HEPSTE. ENTRANCE 1 LEADS FOR ABOUT 30 M TO SUMP 1. THIS IS 21 M LONG TO AN AIRBELL IN A RIFT. A PASSAGE 4 M UP IN THE RIFT LEADS BACK TO THE SECOND ENTRANCE. SUMP 2 CAN BE FOLLOWED FROM THE AIRBELL FOR A TOTAL DISTANCE OF 79 M. 30 M IN FROM THE AIRBELL, A PASSAGE ON THE RIGHT JOINS SUMP 2 IN TUCKS RIFT. TO THE LEFT THE SUMP CAN

BE FOLLOWED FOR 52 M WHILE TO THE RIGHT THE SUMP LEADS TO AN AIRBELL
AFTER 70 M. THE AIRBELL IS 10 M LONG AND IS FOLLOWED BY SUMP 1 WHICH IS 35 M
LONG LEADING TO THE TUCKS RIFT ENTRANCE.
UPSTREAM EAST FROM THE TUCKS RIFT ENTRANCE, A DIVE OF 6 M LEADS TO A
COBBLE SQUEEZE AND A DESCENT OVER A BOULDER PILE TO -3 M IN A LOW
BEDDING, REACHING A SMALL AIRBELL AFTER A FURTHER 6 M. THERE IS A VOICE
CONNECTION BACK TO BASE. AFTER PASSING ANOTHER SQUEEZE, A ROOMIER
PASSAGE IS REACHED AND FOLLOWED FOR 12 M INTO A RIFT AIRBELL (PASSAGE
CLOSES DOWN ABOVE THE WATER). A WAY ON TO THE EAST CLOSES DOWN AFTER 16
M. THE MAIN WAY ON IS 2 M IN DIAMETER AND TURNS THROUGH 90 DEGREES
(SOUTH) AND THEN CONTINUES AT -3 M FOR 20 M TO ANOTHER RIFT AIRBELL. THERE
IS NO DRY WAY ON BUT A DUCK UNDER A FLAKE AND THEN 2 M OF CANAL PASSAGE
LEADS TO SUMP 2. THIS IS OF SMALL DIMENSIONS AND TRENDS SOUTH FOR 22 M TO
ANOTHER AIRBELL WITH A LOW FLOODED BEDDING PLANE HEADING OFF INTO MORE
SPACIOUS PASSAGE. HEADING EAST FOR 14 M IN A PASSAGE 1 M HIGH AND 3 M WIDE
IT SURFACES AFTER A TOTAL OF 36 M FROM THE AIRBELL IN A RIFT. ABOUT 15 M OF
RIFT PASSAGE, 3-4 M HIGH AND 3 M WIDE, THEN LEADS TO SUMP 3 (9 M) WHICH IS
TIGHT WITH A GRAVEL SQUEEZE AT THE START. IT SURFACES IN A POOL WITH TWO
PASSAGES LEADING OFF. A MUDDY DOWNSTREAM PASSAGE ENDS AT A TOO TIGHT
RIFT WHERE WATER DISAPPEARS. UPSTREAM, A CLEAN-WASHED BEDDING PASSAGE
IS FOLLOWED TO A FIRST CHAMBER THEN VIA A LOW DUCK INTO A LARGE PASSAGE.
THIS IS ABOUT 45 M LONG AND CLOSES DOWN INTO A COBBLE CHOKE. THIS HAS
BEEN PASSED FOR ABOUT 60 M AND ENDS IN A TOO TIGHT RIFT.

Ogof Pont Sychryd

Grade 3/4

Grid Ref SN9108 0792   OS Maps 1:50000 sheet 160,
1:25000 Brecon Beacons Central O/L

Altitude : 83 metres

Length : 225 metres

Location   The cave is situated at the bottom of the Sychryd valley. Just before
its confluence with the Afon Mellte, the Afon Sychryd is spanned by a bridge. The
two entrances to the cave are at river level, one almost directly under the bridge
and the other a few metres upstream.
Description   The lower entrance leads via a crawl to the upper entrance where a
sloping rift passage is followed to the start of a crawl on the left. The crawl leads
via two very tight squeezes to a larger passage and then to the Main Chamber
after about 30 m. To the left a large passage leads to a short canal followed by 15
m of dry passage ending in an impenetrable rift. Also to the left of the Main
Chamber, a sandy slope leads to another canal, much longer but eventually
becoming too tight. To the right of the Main Chamber is a series of tight crawls,
one of which leads for some distance but is very unpleasant and wet. Most of the
crawls end in chokes.
Tackle   A wet suit is essential.
History   The cave was first explored by SWCC in 1953. Major extensions made
by BUSS in 1971.
Survey   BUSS in 1972.

Twll Dychryllyd
Alternative name : Blaen Hepste Hole

Grade 3

Grid Ref SN9617 1281   OS Maps 1:50000 sheet 160,
1;25000 Brecon Beacons Central O/L

Length : 100 metres approx.

Location   Situated about 100 m downstream from Blaen Hepste Resurgence at the base of a small cliff.

Description   A small hole leads to a short crawl and a squeeze under a fallen slab. More crawling leads to a long flat-out crawl half full of water which ends at a three-way junction. *To the right are two passages, one is blocked but the other is low and leads to a rift passage followed by another low section which is blocked but diggable.*
The main passage continues to the left from the junction and is larger than before, leading to a streamway. *Upstream a small lake chamber and sump is reached.* **THE SUMP HAS BEEN DIVED TO A CONSTRICTION.** Downstream the water disappears under boulders and is not seen again. A little further on the passage turns right and large slabs block the way but a squeeze over one of the blocks leads to a small chamber with a sand ramp leading up to a wet bedding plane. This can be followed for some way until it becomes too tight.

History   Originally discovered by Severn Valley CC and filled back in. Rediscovered by CDG/SSS in 1990. Survey in Speleogen (SSS Journal) 1990.

Wills Hole
Alternative names : Arthur's Cave, Craig-y-Dinas Cave, Dinas Rock Cave.

Grade 3

Grid Ref SN9147 0802   OS Maps 1:50000 sheet 160,
1:25000 Brecon Beacons Central O/L

Altitude : 102 metres

Length : 393 metres

Location   Situated in the upper part of the Sychryd Gorge. Beyond Bwa Maen the river comes down a steep cascade and the cave is situated in the rock face on the left about half way up the cascade.

Description   An interesting cave with an easy ladder pitch which is well suited for beginners.
The small entrance leads to a short climb down and then to a section of rift passage. At the end of the rift is a pitch. Belay ladder to an iron bar which is wedged across the passage. At the bottom of the pitch, a large passage runs from right to left. To the right the roof quickly lowers to a crawl ending at a small chamber and a boulder choke. To the left the passage continues large to a junction with a stream passage. Downstream the passage ends after about 30 m at a silted sump. **THIS SUMP HAS BEEN DIVED FOR A DISTANCE OF 34 M TO A DEPTH OF 15 M.** Upstream, a large passage ascends for some distance but the roof eventually lowers to a crawl through boulders. The crawl becomes much smaller and ends after a squeeze into a small chamber. There are only a few small side passages throughout the cave, all of which quickly close down.

Tackle   Rift Pitch - 11 m ladder, 6 m belay and lifeline.

History The first recorded exploration of the cave was in 1938.
Survey BUSS in 1972.
WARNING : THE CAVE IS LIABLE TO FLOOD. THE WATER CAN BACK UP TO
FLOOD MOST OF THE CAVE.

Lesser Caves and Sites of Speleological Interest

Birwir Sychryd Resurgence   SN9116 0792
Brecon Road Dig   SN9601 1191
Brecon Road Foxholes   SN9589 1181
Doghole   SN9541 1095
Franks Rift   SN9381 0968
Graig Fawr Foxholes   SN9661 1162
Graig Fawr Sink   SN9188 1341
Hepste Bridge Sinks   SN9475 1132
Hepste Cave No.3   SN9518 1811
Hepste Fawr Road Cave   SN9491 1195
Hepste Fawr Road Sink   SN9492 1195
Hepste Fawr Sink   SN9528 1190
Hepste Fawr Sinks Right-Hand   SN9518 1189
Hepste Flood Resurgence   SN9363 0973
Hepste Foxholes   SN9379 0965
Hepste Main Resurgence   SN9360 0973
Hepste Rift No.2   SN9518 1185
Llwyn Celyn Spring   SN9472 1133
Llygad Cynnon Resurgence   SN9524 0774
Lower Cil-Hepste Falls Rising   SN9268 0989
Middle Hepste Cave   SN9381 0966
Middle Hepste Main Sink   SN9389 0969
Middle Hepste Northeast Cave   SN9386 0969
Middle Hepste Rising   SN9431 1107
Middle Hepste Sink   SN9381 0966
Middle Hepste Southeast Dig   SN9389 0968
Middle Hepste Southwest Dig   SN9382 0968
Moel Penderyn Stream Sink   SN9377 0965
Mynydd-y-Glog   SN9700 0900
Nant Cwrier Bridge Rising   SN9748 1396
Ogof Dan Gi   SN9233 1235
Ogof Fawr   SN9853 0961
Ogof Fawr Dig   SN9853 0960
Ogof Faswr Flood Rising   SN9529 0784
Ogof Foel   SN9385 0875
Ogof Gorllewinol Cader Fawr   SN9751 1234
Ogof Hepste No.2   SN9518 1181
Ogof Pioden   SN9511 1409
Ogof Pwll-y-Dram Cave   SN9363 0972
Ogof Sulgwyn   SN9292 1292
Ogof-y-Ci Mawr   SN9319 1242
Ogof yr Uwd Lwyd   SN9738 1236
Pant Cefn-y-Ffordd Sink   SN9427 0858

Pant-y-Hwyn Cave   SN9216 1240
Penderyn Church Sink   SN9428 0858
Penderyn Quarry Cave   SN9586 0900
Petes Pot   SN9300 1200
Pwll Coed-y-Rhaiadr Sink   SN9164 1190
Pwll Heol Brychan Sink   SN9489 1068
Pwll Hepste   SN9518 1187
Pwll Mawr Sink   SN9541 1095
Pwll-y-Eithin   SN9491 0797
Roses Rift   SN9382 0968
Tarddiant Hepste Sink   SN9367 0970
Terrace cave   SN9160 0806
Tir-Duweunydd North Sink   SN9471 1177
Tir-Duweunydd South Sink   SN9474 1173
Tir-Duweunydd Well   SN9489 1180
Tir-Duweunydd Well Cave   SN9485 1189
Tir-Duweunydd Well Sink   SN9489 1179
Tor-y-Foel Spring   SN9417 0899
Twyn Du Swallet   SN9599 1160
Upper Hepste Heol-las Dig   SN9600 1268
Upper Hepste Heol-las Resurgence   SN9604 1268
Upper Hepste Heol-las Sink   SN9568 1231
Upper Hepste Main Sink   SN9541 1208
Upper Hepste Neuadd Hole   SN9527 1191
Upper Hepste Resurgence Cave   SN9632 1283
Upper hepste Tir-Mawr Sink   SN9516 1219
Upper Hepste Tir-Mawr Upper Sink   SN9544 1212
Upper Hepste Tir yr Onneu Sink   SN9647 1286

6. Ystradfellte Area

Bridge Cave Grade 2
Alternative name : Ogof Nedd Fechan

Grid Ref SN 9116 1400 OS Maps 1:50 000 sheet 160,
1:25 000 Brecon Beacons Central O/L

Altitude : 308 metres

Length : 311 metres

Location Follow the road which leads from Pont Nedd Fechan towards
Ystradfellte. After a few kilometres take the turning on the left towards Berthlwyd
Farm. About 800 metres past the farm, a steep track leads down on the left to a
bridge over the Nedd Fechan river. The entrance to the cave is in a large
depression on the near bank to the left of the bridge.
Access Permission to visit the cave must be obtained from Blaen-nedd-Isaf
Farm (a little further down the road). The farmer charges a small goodwill fee.
Description This cave is actually part of the nearby Little Neath River Cave to
which it is connected by a long sump. It is a good cave for beginners providing a
relatively safe and interesting preview of an active river system.
A wide low entrance at the bottom of the depresssion leads to a dry crawling,
sometimes stooping, passage which eventually leads to a boulder choke. The
choke is passed on the left-hand side and although it appears reasonably stable,
care should be taken. Beyond, a fast flowing stream is found in a narrow
meandering streamway and leads, after about 20 m, into the very large Main
Passage. *On the right is the lofty West Passage which leads to a choke where
a waterfall can be seen when the level of the river outside is high.* Continuing
down the Main Passage, the now enlarged stream takes up the whole width of
the passage and flows between steep walls. *A high level inlet passage on the
right leads for about 27 m via a duck to Sump 1a which is 2.7 m long. This is
followed a short distance later by Sump 2a which is 0.9 m long and then Sump
3a which is 1.2 m long. After a further 12 m the final sump, Sump 4a is met.*
THIS HAS BEEN DIVED FOR 45 M VIA TWO SQUEEZES TO A LOW BEDDING PLANE.
Just before the point where the Main Passage decreases in size, *a climb up on
the right-hand wall leads to the Bridge, a large oblong boulder which spans
the width of the Main Passage. There are also a few calcite formations and a
small blind passage.* Downstream the Main Passage gradually becomes lower
and narrower, between calcited walls, until it ends in an 18 m long sump (not
free-diveable) which connects with the Little Neath River Cave.
History The first recorded exploration was by T.S.J.Braithwaite in the 1930's.
The boulder choke was passed in 1947 by SWCC. Survey by UBSS in 1970.

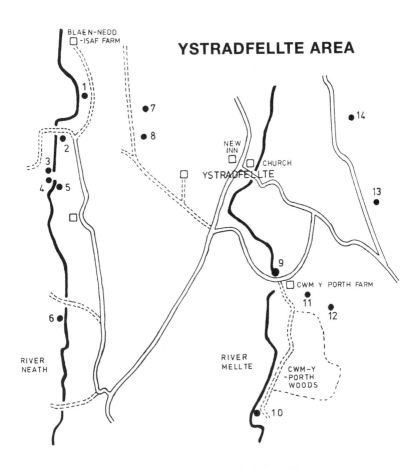

YSTRADFELLTE AREA

1. LITTLE NEATH RIVER CAVE
2. BRIDGE CAVE
3. CWM PWLL Y RHYD
4. WHITE LADY CAVE
5. TOWN DRAIN
6. OGOF CAS
7. Y GWAL
8. THE HOLE BY THE WALL
9. PORTH YR OGOF
10. OGOF GLAN MELLTE
11. OGOF COEDEN PROP
12. OGOF FFYNNON
13. PULPIT HOLE
14. OGOF GARREG FAWR

Cwm Pwll-y-Rhyd
Alternative name : Deep Pit Cave

Grade 3

Grid Ref SN 9114 1375   OS Maps 1:50 000 sheet 160,
1:25 000 Brecon Beacons Central O/L

Altitude : 305 metres

Length : 300 m + (inc.White Lady Cave)

Location   The cave is a well known landmark and is marked on OS maps.
Follow the river bed downstream from Bridge Cave until it suddenly disappears
into the chasm of Cwm Pwll-y-Rhyd. In summer the river bed is usually dry.
Access   See Bridge Cave.
Description   This cave, together with White Lady Cave, forms part of the
underground course of the Nedd Fechan.
A climb down into the chasm and to the right leads to deep water and the 27 m
sump which connects to White Lady Cave. A small passage under the right hand
wall is the connection to White Lady II, 245 metres of open passages with a small
stream. However, this passage usually becomes blocked during the winter and it
may be necessary to dig it out. There is also a short dry upper series above the
chasm.
On the opposite side of the chasm, a climb up boulders leads to a short section
of lofty passage with some formations in the roof. A climb up leads to an exit high
above the river while a crawl at floor level leads to a lower exit.
History   The entrance part of the cave has probably always been known but
was surveyed in 1959 by SWCC.

Cwm-y-Porth Woods Caves

Grade 1/2

Grid Ref SN 9280-9304 1151-1211   OS Maps 1:50 000 sheet 160,
1:25 000 Brecon Beacons Central O/L

Altitude : 274 metres

Length : up to 73 metres

Location   Take the track which runs south from opposite the car park at Porth-
yr-Ogof to Cwm-y-Porth Farm. The woods start just past the farm on the left-
hand side.
Description   There are a large number of caves scattered throughout the wood.
These vary from small holes to large cavernous entrances leading to short
sections of generally small passage.

Ffynnon Garreg Fawr
Alternative name : Rover's Cave, Ogof Garreg Fawr

Grid Ref SN 9379 1387	OS Maps 1:50 000 sheet 160,
	1:25 000 Brecon Beacons Central O/L

Altitude : 302 metres

Length : 457 metres

Location   The entrance is a small rising near Garreg Fawr Farm on the Penderyn to Mellte Castle road.
Access   The farm uses this resurgence as a domestic water supply and will not allow visitors to the cave under any circumstances.
Description   The cave consists of a system of tight and wet passages which have been followed for a considerable distance, bypassing several sumps. The known passages are immature and no sign of a larger fossil system has been found. It is certain to flood after heavy rain.
History   The cave was first explored by SWCC in 1955 and major extensions were made in 1965.

Little Neath River Cave   Grade 4

Grid Ref SN 9118 1420	OS Maps 1:50 000 sheet 160,
	1:25 000 Brecon Beacons Central O/L

Altitude : 304 metres

Length : 7,855 metres

Location   The entrance is situated in the east bank of the Afon Nedd Fechan about 200 m upstream of Bridge Cave. It is at the base of a small cliff and takes water from the river at most times of the year. An alternative dry entrance is not recommended due to loose boulders.
Access   See Bridge Cave
Description   One of the most popular and sporting caves in South Wales. It is an extensive system of active and fossil passages with lots of interest.
The low entrance gives access to a flat-out crawl and then hands and knees crawl in water. It follows through many right-angled turns until a duck under a low arch leads to a larger and more lofty passage. *To the left is Blaen Nedd Isaf Passage, a wet inlet,* but the way on is downstream to the right. The passage soon becomes narrower and then a small waterfall drops into a pool. The usual way on is over a flat boulder on the left and then on downstream through a tight wet squeeze (there is also a high level route through boulders). Beyond the squeeze, a climb up over a rockfall which hides another branch of the Blaen Nedd Isaf Passage, leads to a canyon type passage with a smooth floor. A large dry oxbow leads off on the left but the streamway continues at stooping height. At the point where it becomes difficult to follow the stream, a climb on the right leads to a dry bypass. *Having rejoined the stream on the other side, a stalagmite bank rises on the left and leads to the Canal Bypass. This is not to be confused with the stal bank passed earlier which only leads to a short passage ending in a too tight bedding plane.*
Following the stream, the passage becomes much lower and then gains height

as it enters the large Sand Chamber. The stream follows the left wall while to the right is a large sand bank leading to the Mud Hall. At the far end of Sand Chamber another stream enters from the Bridge Cave sump (Sump 1) on the right, to join up with the Little Neath stream to flow under the left-hand wall. This is the start of The Canal, a 150 m bedding plane crawl in flowing water which can rise to the roof in wet weather.

The Canal Bypass can be followed to avoid the Canal and begins as walking passage over shallow gour pools. The roof gradually lowers to a crawl until a low arch leads to a larger dry passage. This is followed until a small stream enters from the left. *The stream comes from the North East Inlet Series and there are some fine gours a few metres along this passage. To avoid spoiling the gours, access to the North East Inlets should be made via the main Bypass passage for a few more metres and then turning left into a passage which rejoins the other passage beyond the gours. The North East Inlets are an extensive series of both wet and dry passages and involves a lot of crawling.*

Continuing along the Canal Bypass a waterfall, which is sometimes quite impressive, issues from the right-hand wall. Further along the passage the stream turns sharp right under a low opening but straight ahead is a slippery calcite climb which leads, past a small curtain, into a large dry passage. This passage contains a few calcite formations and leads to Junction Chamber. This part of the cave is instantly recognisable from the huge boulders which have fallen from the roof. The Canal enters from the right but the way on is between the boulders to the left and into the Main Stream Passage which assumes large proportions, about 10 m x 10m.

The main stream is fairly shallow in normal conditions and spreads across most of the passage width. Along the right-hand wall is a large steep mud bank. *A short way along this mud bank is a climb up leading to a stony crawl and then to the start of Genesis Gallery. To the right is the 3D Maze, an area of rectangular blocks. A route through the maze, which is difficult to find and involves two tight squeezes, leads to the Old World Series where there are some fine calcite decorations. A large passage is followed to Gooseberry Pot which is 6 m deep. The way on is found by traversing halfway down the pitch into an oxbow. The last 60 m of this passage is a low crawl in mud and over sharp rocks.*

Back in Genesis Gallery, by keeping to the left wall leads to some well decorated avens and then a crawl and a squeeze lead to a wet aven. This is Genesis Inlet and a 6 m maypole is required to enter a series of well decorated avens and passages. This route requires a lot of climbing to reach a large chamber which marks the end of the series.

Continuing down the mainstream passage *a climb up on the left enters a small passage which runs back the other way to emerge high up above the stream opposite Genesis Gallery.* Downstream the water enters a canyon type passage at the large Bouncing Boulder Hall. *At the far end of the hall is the 10 m maypole entrance to the High Level Series.* Beyond the end of the hall, the Main Stream Passage roof gradually lowers to a duck which can sump in wet weather. This can be bypassed by climbing into the roof, just before the duck, and following a tube which goes over the top and drops back into the stream on the other side. Beyond, the passage is quite wide but mostly of stooping height. After some distance the roof descends to meet the water at Sump 2 (Bridge Cave Sump being Sump 1). To the left of the sump is a muddy and slippery climb into Gryn Fawr Passage which contains a fine calcite pool.

SUMP 2 AND BEYOND IS ONLY ACCESSIBLE TO DIVERS AND STARTS WITH A DIVE OF

37 M WHICH IS CONSTRICTED AT ITS DOWNSTREAM END. A SINGLE CHAMBER 10 M LONG THEN LEADS TO SUMP 3 WHICH IS 57 M LONG FOLLOWED BY 45 M OF ROOMY STREAMWAY. SUMP 4 IS 38 M LONG. BEYOND, IT IS POSSIBLE TO CLIMB UP IN SEVERAL PLACES TO A COMPLEX SERIES OF HIGH LEVEL PASSAGES INCLUDING THE MOST SPECTACULAR HIGH LEVEL PASSAGE IN THE CAVE - THE NEW WORLD PASSAGE. THIS ALSO PROVIDES A BYPASS TO SUMP 5 (36 M), BOTH TERMINATING IN LAKE CHAMBER AND SUMP 6 WHICH IS 90 M LONG. A SHORT PASSAGE IS THEN FOLLOWED TO SUMP 7 WHICH IS AGAIN 90 M LONG WITH A SMALL AIRBELL AT 30 M. AFTER A FURTHER 182 M THE TERMINAL SUMP IS MET. THIS HAS BEEN DIVED FOR A DISTANCE OF 150 M AND A DEPTH OF 27 M AND ENDS IN BOULDERS.

Tackle   A wetsuit is essential. In winter the water in the entrance series is icy cold.

History   The cave was first explored by the UBSS in 1967. Survey -   An extract from U.B.S.S.Proceedings containing full description and survey was published as a separate booklet in 1973.

WARNING : THE CAVE IS LIABLE TO SEVERE AND RAPID FLOODING. As water from the river flows directly into the entrance it can become impassable after rain. It is best to avoid the cave in winter.

Ogof Cas

Grid Ref SN 9117 1243   OS Maps 1:50 000 sheet 160,
                                    1:25 000 Brecon Beacons Central O/L

Altitude : 233 metres

Length : 106 metres approx.

Location   Situated in the bed of the Nedd Fechan river about 1200 metres downstream from White Lady Cave. The entrance can become blocked with flood debris.

Description   This cave is probably a flood rising for the Pant Mawr system. It is totally flooded and is only accessible to divers.

A SUMP WHICH IS 73 M LONG LEADS TO AN AIRBELL. SUMP 2 FOLLOWS AND IS 26 M LONG WITH A SQUEEZE AND A LOW SECTION BEFORE IT ASCENDS TO A LARGER PASSAGE, 6 M WIDE AND JUST OVER 1 M HIGH.

History   Explored by members of the CDG over a number of years.

Ogof Coeden Prop   Grade 2

Grid Ref SN 9323 1226   OS Maps 1:50 000 sheet 160,
                                    1:25 000 Brecon Beacons Central O/L

Altitude : 312 metres

Length : 60 metres approx.

Location   Follow the track which leads from the car park at Porth-yr-Ogof to Cwm-y-Porth farm. Just past the farm a stile on the left leads to a path which runs up the side of the woods. The path turns sharp left and right around the wood and then leads onto the moor. Head towards a solitary hawthorn tree which marks a line of depressions. The entrance is situated in the side of the shakehole which is nearest the river and to the left of the tree.

Description   The small entrance leads to a choice of two ways on. Straight ahead is a crawl while to the right a drop down leads to a passage which is later joined by the crawl. The route through the cave is at high level over a number of blind shafts which at times can be full of water.

The cave is typical of shakehole development in the area and care should be taken as the rock is very sharp and brittle. There are loose boulders and stones above most of the shafts.

History   The cave was first explored by SWCC in 1947.

Ogof Ffynnon

Grade 3/4

Grid Ref SN 9340 1202   OS Maps 1:50 000 sheet 160,
1:25 000 Brecon Beacons Central O/L

Altitude : 320 metres

Length : 300 metres +

Location   The entrance is situated in the same line of depressions as Ogof Coeden Prop. Follow the line away from the river and the cave is situated in the bottom of the last large sinkhole before reaching the forest. A small stream sinks into the entrance.

Description   The impressive entrance leads to a passage going left and formed between steeply dipping beds. At the far end, a squeeze down through a small hole leads to a descending route through boulders to a slot. An awkward climb down the slot drops into a small passage. To the left (with back to the climb) an excavated crawl leads via a couple of squeezes to Bell Chamber with a descending boulder floor and a few nice calcite decorations on the right-hand wall. On the far side of the chamber is a high level inlet passage which leads to two avens which are about 15 m high.

To the right at the bottom of the slot another crawl can be followed to a tight squeeze into the large Main Chamber which lies below the entrance passage. At the far end, the water from the entrance stream drops down through a very unstable boulder choke which is constantly on the move. A wet hole in the bottom of the choke leads to a small chamber where a squeeze gives access to the top of a boulder slope. Descending the slope the cave changes character with good solid walls and roof. Straight ahead and up a sand slope leads to an excavated crawl and a rift chamber while to the left, before the slope, gives access to a clean-washed phreatic crawl. The passage turns left, descending gently, and becomes progressively more muddy before reaching a sump. At times of exceptional drought or prolonged freezing conditions the sump dries up and it is possible to reach a chamber and continuing passage which eventually ends in mud.

History   The cave was first explored by SWCC in 1947. After digging operations, SSS discovered the left-hand series in 1977 and the right-hand series beyond the Main Chamber in 1978.

WARNING : THERE ARE MANY LOOSE BOULDERS THROUGHOUT THE CAVE AND THE BOULDER CHOKE INTO THE RIGHT-HAND SERIES IS CONSTANTLY ON THE MOVE.

Ogof Glan Mellte

Grade 1

Grid Ref SN 9266 1168   OS Maps 1:50 000 sheet 160,
1:25 000 Brecon Beacons Central O/L

Altitude: 230 metres

Length: 45 metres

Location   Follow the left-hand bank of the River Mellte downstream from the Porth-yr-Ogof resurgence intil it flows through a small gorge. The cave is situated in this gorge on the left. A small stream issues from the cave and the entrance is just above.
Description   A low entrance hole leads to a narrow meandering streamway. There are no side passages and the cave ends in a low section which becomes too tight. There are a few small calcite decorations.

Ogof Gwdihw

Grade 2

Grid Ref SN 9106 1316   OS Maps 1:50 000 sheet 160,
1:25 000 Brecon Beacons Central O/L

Length: 48 metres

Location   Situated in the east bank of the Afon Nedd Fechan about 430 m south of Cwm Pwll y Rhyd.
Description   A small cave forming part of an oxbow to the main river. The small entrance leads to a low bedding cave with a boulder floor. After about 35 m the passage briefly assumes larger proportions before returning to its original size and ending in boulders.
History   Discovered in 1980 by Croydon CC. Survey Unit Two in 1982.
WARNING: THE CAVE IS LIABLE TO FLOOD.

Ogof Gwib

Grade 3

Grid Ref SN 9104 1337   OS Maps 1:50 000 sheet 160,
1:25 000 Brecon Beacons Central O/L

Length: 70 metres approx.

Location   Situated on the opposite side of the river and about 10 m downstream from Ogof Igam-Ogam.
Description   About 60 metres of very constricted passage leads to a very tight sump. **THE SUMP IS 3 M LONG AND LEADS TO A FURTHER 6 M OF DRY PASSAGE BEFORE BECOMING PROHIBITIVELY TIGHT. A TINY STREAM FLOWS INTO A SMALLER, PARALLEL, SIDE RIFT BUT THERE IS NO POSSIBILITY OF FURTHER PROGRESS.**
History   Sump dived by M.Stewart.

Ogof Igam-Ogam

Grid Ref SN 9104 1337   OS Maps 1:50 000 sheet 160,
1:25 000 Brecon Beacons Central O/L

Length: 520 metres
Vertical Range: 30 metres

Location   The cave is situated on the west bank of the Afon Nedd Fechan about 300 metres downstream from White Lady Cave. The entrance is a small phreatic tube.

Access   Permission to visit this cave must be obtained from the farmer at Dyffrn-Nedd Farm.

Description   This is essentially a divers cave as only the first 65 m is accessible without diving equipment. The passage to Sump 1 is generally tight with squeezes and a couple of sharp bends. **SUMP 1 (22 M) IS A 0.6 M HIGH PHREATIC TUBE VIA TWO SMALL AIRBELLS TO A 2.5 M POT GIVING ACCESS TO A LOW ARCH AND CONTINUATION OF THE SUMP. BEWARE OF LOOSE ROCKS ON THE FLOOR ROLLING INTO THE GAP AT THE BOTTOM OF THE POT. 6 M FURTHER ON THE PASSAGE COMES UP TO AIR IN A RIFT PASSAGE. THE SUMP IS NORMALLY DIVED FEET FIRST. THE RIFT IS ABOUT 13 M LONG AND ENDS AT A 2 M STEP-DOWN TO SUMP 2. SUMP 2 IS A STRAIGHTFORWARD DIVE OF 21 M FOLLOWED BY A DUCK AND A 17 M CRAWL TO SUMP 3. SUMP 3 IS JUST 3 M LONG FOLLOWED BY A SERIES OF CLIMB DOWNS INTO A LARGE BREAKDOWN CHAMBER, SUZUKI CHAMBER.
A SQUEEZE AT THE BOTTOM OF THE CHAMBER TO THE RIGHT LEADS TO A CRAWL AND THEN WALKING PASSAGE TO A JUNCTION WITH A LARGER PASSAGE. TO THE LEFT, BELOW STALS, LEADS TO A LARGE PASSAGE WHICH CAN BE FOLLOWED FOR ABOUT 60 M. TO THE RIGHT, THE PASSAGE CONTINUES DOWNSTREAM, SOMETIMES LARGE WALKING SIZE AND SOMETIMES ON HANDS AND KNEES, FOR NEARLY 200 M TO SUMP 4 WHICH HAS BEEN DIVED FOR ABOUT 7 M.**

History   Discovered and explored by CCC in 1988. Survey in Descent (83) 1988.

Ogof O'Flaen-y-Waun   Grade 3

Grid Ref SN 8951 1605   OS Maps 1:50 000 sheet 160,
1:25 000 Brecon Beacons Central O/L

Altitude: 429 metres

Length: 180 metres approx.

Location   Situated on Pant Mawr to the west of the Nedd Fechan valley. The entrance is a small sinkhole situated about 800 metres east of Pant Mawr Pot and is difficult to find.

Description   A drop down through a hole leads to a crawl and after a short distance the stream disappears into a low bedding. A muddy crawl on the right bypasses the bedding and eventually drops back into the stream at the other end. The passage slowly becomes wider and a short side passage can be entered through boulders on the right. The main passage continues and is large enough to stand in but gradually becomes lower and wider until the stream sinks in a low bedding blocked by stones.

History   The cave was first explored by SWCC in 1970. Minor extensions by WSG. Survey in Descent (117) 1994.

Ogof Triachwech

Grade 1

Grid Ref SN 9013 1602   OS Maps 1:50 000 sheet 160,
1:25 000 Brecon Beacons Central O/L

Altitude: 415 metres

Length: 60 metres

Location   Situated beside the Nant y Moch valley just south of Fan Fraith. The two entrances to the cave are in a boulder pile and there is a small resurgence nearby.
Description   Both entrances lead to a single, low, passage containing a small stream. The passage ends in a flat out crawl which becomes too tight where the passage splits into two.
History   First explored by WSG in 1972.

Pant Mawr Pot

Grade 3

Grid Ref SN 8909 1612   OS Maps 1:50 000 sheet 160,
1:25 000 Brecon Beacons Central O/L

Altitude: 436 metres

Length: 1152 metres
Vertical Range: 97 metres

Location   The entrance shaft is situated in a deep depression on Pant Mawr to the west of the Nedd Fechan valley. The easiest approach however is from the SWCC hut at Penwyllt and is about one hours walk. Follow the old tramroad which goes past OFD top entrance until it ends at an old quarry a little way past Pwll Byffre. A track to the left of the quarry leads to a stone wall which is followed east to an iron gate. The entrance to the cave is situated on the moor on the other side of the gate and can just be seen on a clear day by looking straight ahead and slightly to the left. The depression has a fence around it but is difficult to find in wet or misty weather.
The cave can also be approached from the Nedd Fechan but please note the access arrangements.
Access   The caving rights over Pant Mawr moor are vested in the SWCC and persons wishing to visit the cave should apply for written permission to the Hon.Secretary SWCC.
Description   A fine cave of large proportions which contains a sizeable stream and some fine calcite decorations.
The impressive entrance shaft requires a ladder or rope which can be belayed to rawlbolts on the ledge immediately above the pitch or to an iron stake just outside the fence. If descending from the ledge it is advisable to use a handline from the stake to the ledge. The first part of the pitch is against the wall but then opens out to a fine free-hang and lands in a large chamber with a stream flowing from north to south. Upstream the passage, with fine phreatic shelving, can be

PLEASE DISPLAY THIS TICKET IN YOUR VEHICLE WINDSCREEN

Parking at Porth yr Ogof

The attendant provides some supervision of the car park but VEHICLES ARE LEFT AT THEIR OWNERS' RISK and the National Park Authority accepts no liability for damage or theft.

BRECON BEACONS
NATIONAL PARK

PARC CENEDLAETHOL
BANNAU BRYCHEINIOG

CAR OR MOTORBIKE
day or part of day

£2

Charge includes VAT
Ticket valid on day of issue only.............
11-5-97
....

TICKET No.   6005

See over

The magnificent waterfalls are set in steep-sided valleys where unstable or wet rocks can be very dangerous. Keep to the waymarked paths and take special care if the ground is at all slippery.

Please:

▲ keep dogs under close control

▲ guard against all risk of fire

▲ take litter home

BRECON BEACONS NATIONAL PARK

Brecon Beacons National Park Authority

7 Glamorgan Street, Brecon, Powys, LD3 7DP

Telephone (01874) 624437

followed to a waterfall and then a climb up leads to a bedding plane crawl which
becomes too tight to progress.

Downstream, the large passage is followed for about 120 m to the First Boulder
Choke. This completely blocks the passage but can be passed via a hole on the
right-hand side. After a short distance is the Second Boulder Choke and this is
bypassed by an oxbow on the right. The oxbow rejoins the main passage which
continues over large boulders, past a fine stal curtain, to the Third Boulder
Choke. A climb up through an obvious hole leads to the Great Hall where the
passage takes on much larger proportions. *To the left of the Great Hall is The
Chapel which contains some fine helictites. To the right a wide passage leads
to a small inlet stream issuing from a small hole. A crawl through the hole,
bearing left, enters a high passage. A climb up to the left leads to The Vestry
while a climb over stal to the right leads to the decorated Organ Loft.*
Continuing along the main passage from the Great Hall, the stream is again met
and there are several mud covered calcite formations on the right-hand wall. A
mud bank stretches up to the left and a passage known as the Dead End leads
off. This has been periodically dug over a number of years and can be followed
along a comfortable sandy crawl for some distance. Further along the main
passage is a forceful flow of water entering from the right-hand wall and known
as the Fire Hydrant. The source of this water is presumably the small stream
passage which can be entered via a 2.5 m climb above the hydrant and which
can be followed for about 80 m to where falling water can be heard but is too
tight to continue.

The main passage then gradually narrows down and ends at a sump. **THE SUMP
HAS BEEN DIVED FOR A DISTANCE OF 122 M VIA AN AIRBELL AFTER 27 M. THE
UNDERWATER PASSAGE AT THE END IS CHOKED.**

Tackle   Entrance Pitch
           (from ledge) 15 m ladder or rope, 2 rawlbolts & lifeline
           15 m handline for descending to the ledge
           (from stake) 30 m ladder or rope, 3 m belay and lifeline

History   The cave was first explored by the South Wales section of the Wessex
Caving Club in 1937. Survey by CRG in 1959.

Porth-yr-Ogof   Grade 3/4
Alternative name: White Horse Cave, Porth Mawr   11 mAy 199?

Grid Ref SN 9281 1241   OS Maps 1: 50 000 sheet 160,
                                         1:25 000 Brecon Beacons Central O/L

Altitude : 229 metres

Length : 2,220 metres

Location   The cave is a well known tourist spot and is marked on OS maps.
From Ystradfellte take the road towards Pont Nedd Fechan. After less than 800
metres, a single track road leads off on the left by an old milk churn stand. The
road descends to where a large car park is situated above the cave.

Description   The cave is an impressive horizontal river system which forms part
of the course of the Afon Mellte. There are no fewer than 15 entrances. The cave
is used by many youth organisations and adventure centres but is not really an
ideal cave for novices. The water is very cold, deep in places, and has claimed

many lives during past years. IN PARTICULAR, THE RESURGENCE IS VERY DANGEROUS AND EXIT VIA THIS ROUTE SHOULD BE AVOIDED BY ALL EXCEPT THE VERY EXPERIENCED. IT SHOULD NEVER BE ATTEMPTED, EVEN BY THE STRONGEST OF SWIMMERS, WITHOUT A FLOATATION DEVICE. THERE IS A STRONG UNDERTOW WHICH CAN DRAG THE UNWARY SWIMMER UNDER THE WATER WHERE THEY CAN BECOME ENTANGLED IN OLD TREE BRANCHES, ETC.

The Main Entrance is impressive. Situated at the foot of the cliff immediately below the car park, it is nearly 5 m high and over 17 m wide, making it the largest cave entrance in Wales. Straight ahead the passage, of equally large proportions, is strewn with small boulders until it meets deep water at the White Horse Pool. From here the impressive river passage turns right and continues in very deep and very cold water for approximately 60 m, eventually becoming shallower in the Great Bedding Cave which in places is over 30 m wide. The water gradually becomes deeper again, passing alternative entrances, to end at the final lake. Daylight can be seen from the resurgence ahead (please note warning at beginning of Description). There are three other small entrances near the resurgence.

Back at the Main Entrance, a large dry passage on the right leads through flood debris to the Right-Hand Series, beneath two aven entrances, and then to the Great Bedding Cave. About 15 m along this passage, a smaller passage on the right leads to The Creek, a fine canyon passage, which again emerges in the Great Bedding Cave. *To the right of The Creek is a series of passages called The Maze. There is also a series of high-level oxbows, one of which leads to Hywell's Grotto which once contained some fine calcite decorations. There are two small entrances in the cliff outside the Main Entrance which lead directly into The Maze.*

Two passages on the left of the Main Entrance Passage lead to the Upper Stream Passage. Downstream this passage can be followed to Sump 5 which is an awkward duck of 3 m with only a couple of centimetres of air space. The sump can be passed in dry weather to an oval shaped passage which leads to the White Horse Pool. Upstream, a fine section of passage with fast flowing water leads to Sump 3 and the Tradesman's Entrance on the left.

THE UPPER CAVE, WHICH IS BEYOND SUMP 3, IS ONLY ACCESSIBLE TO DIVERS. IT IS DEVELOPED ON TWO DIFFERENT LEVELS. THERE ARE FOUR INSIGNIFICANT STATIC SUMPS ON THE FIRST LEVEL. UC SUMPS 1 & 2 ARE BOTH LESS THAN 2 M LONG AND CAN BE BYPASSED. UC SUMP 3 IS 20 M LONG TO A CHOKE AND UC SUMP 4 WHICH IS A BRANCH OFF SUMP 3 ALSO CHOKES.

FROM THE TRADESMAN'S ENTRANCE, SUMP 3 IS 28 M LONG TO AN AIRBELL AND THEN SUMP 2 IS 3 M TO THE UPPER ENTRANCE. SUMP 1 IS THE UPSTREAM CONTINUATION FROM THE AIRBELL AND LEADS TO THE UPPER CAVE AND TOP ENTRANCE.

AN EASIER WAY INTO THE UPPER CAVE IS VIA THE TOP ENTRANCE WHICH IS SITUATED ABOUT 60 M UPSTREAM FROM THE UPPER ENTRANCE. A DIVE OF 31 M BEARING LEFT AT A JUNCTION LEADS TO THE UPPER CAVE. STRAIGHT AHEAD AT THE JUNCTION AND 8 M FURTHER ON IS A FOUR WAY JUNCTION WHERE THE SUMPS FROM THE TRADESMAN'S ENTRANCE ENTER. BY GOING LEFT FOR 32 M AIRSPACE IS AGAIN REACHED IN THE UPPER CAVE.

14 M BACK FROM THE UPPER CAVE, A SUBMERGED PASSAGE ENTERS THE CONTINUATION OF THE MAINSTREAM. AFTER 6 M, A POT 4.5 M DEEP LEADS TO ESSER'S PASSAGE WHERE THERE IS A SMALL OXBOW. CONTINUING THE DIVE FOR

ANOTHER 58 M VIA ANOTHER POT LEADS TO AN AVEN AIRBELL. 3 M FORWARD AND A NARROW AIRBELL IS FOLLOWED BY A 5 M DIVE TO A LARGER AIRBELL AND DRY LAND. A 20 M FURTHER DIVE VIA AN AIRBELL ENDS AT AN AIRBELL WHICH IS HOPELESSLY CHOKED.

Tackle   A wet suit is essential if following the Main River Passage.
Aven Entrance to Right-Hand Series - 15 m ladder or rope, belay and lifeline
History   The cave has been known for centuries and there are many references to it in old travellers tales. Survey UBSS Proc.Vol.12, No.2, 1970
WARNING : THE CAVE IS LIABLE TO SEVERE FLOODING.

Pwll y Coeden Gnau   Grade 3

Grid Ref SN 9113 1245   OS Maps 1:50 000 sheet 160,
                                            1:25 000 Brecon Beacons Central O/L

Altitude : 262 metres

Length : 213 metres approx.

Location   The cave is situated in a forest on the western bank of the Afon Nedd Fechan and is not easy to find. The entrance is a small depression, not far inside the forest boundary, and almost opposite Dyffryn Nedd Farm and almost directly above Ogof Cas.
Description   The muddy entrance shaft (a handline can be useful) leads to a small chamber. From here, two shafts descend in the floor. The one to the left is blind and about 6 m deep, but the one to the right can be free-climbed for about 12 m to a muddy passage. To the right, a muddy crawl followed by a climb up through muddy boulders leads to a loose scree slope which ascends to Toot Chamber. An obvious passage leads on to a small chamber which is choked at the far end. However, by climbing a slope on the right brings you out halfway up the wall in Root Chamber. A short traverse then gives access to a passage which can be followed past some small calcite decorations to Pinnacle Chamber from which there is no way on.
To the left from the bottom of the entrance shaft, the muddy passage is followed for a few metres to a hole under the right-hand wall. This leads to Canal Passage and about 90 metres of very tight wet crawl. Beyond the hole, the main passage becomes a crawl and then enters an aven about 6 m high. Straight on leads to another aven followed by a crawl ending at a boulder choke. To the right at the first aven is the Sandy Crawl, about 30 m of comfortable crawling passage heading straight into the hillside. This ends at a large run-in choke which has been dug periodically without success.
History   First explored by the SWCC in 1962. Extended by CCC and WSG. Survey in WSG Bulletin 7 (12) 1972.

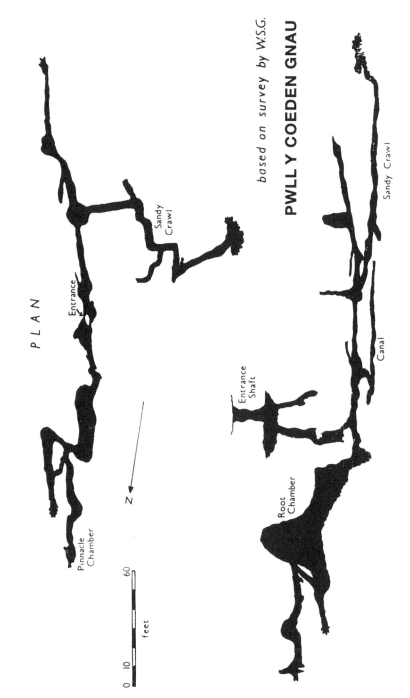

PLAN

PWLL Y COEDEN GNAU

based on survey by W.S.G.

Entrance

Sandy Crawl

Pinnacle Chamber

N

feet

0   10   60

Entrance Shaft

Root Chamber

Canal

Sandy Crawl

Pulpit Hole   Grade 3
Alternative name: Gwaen Cefn-y-Garreg Pothole

Grid Ref SN 9408 1304   OS Maps 1:50 000 sheet 160,
                                              1:25 000 Brecon Beacons Central O/L

Altitude : 366 metres

Length : 106 metres

Location   The road from Penderyn to Mellte Castle passes through a forested
area, by the junction with the road which leads down to Porth-yr-Ogof. On the
right, the forest rises on the slopes of Gwaen Cefn-y-Garreg. Towards the far end
of the forest, a stile leads to a path which up through the trees and directly to the
cave. The entrance is hidden from view in a depression just beyond the top edge
of the forest.
Description   An interesting cave which has developed close to the surface of the
hillside and shows many features of typical shakehole development in the area.
The large entrance leads immediately to an impressive chamber with a large
cross-rift. *The rift goes down to the right, between fluted walls developed by
surface percolation, but soon becomes very narrow and blocked by boulders.*
Crossing over the top of the rift, immediately opposite the entrance, and then
past a shaft leads to a muddy climb up into a small passage. The passage leads
to a squeeze into a small chamber with deep glutinous red mud. An unpleasant
crawl through the mud leads to a large muddy shaft where great care must be
taken. A ladder is required but it is difficult to find a good belay. At the bottom of
the shaft, a small passage with a stream can be followed for a short distance.
Tackle   8 m ladder, belay and lifeline.
History   The first recorded exploration was by T.Braithwaite in 1936.

The Hole by the Wall   Grade 2
Alternative name: Mutton Pot

Grid Ref SN 9209 1351   OS Maps 1:50 000 sheet 160,
                                              1:25 000 Brecon Beacons Central O/L

Altitude : 322 metres

Length : 15 metres

Location   From the Pont Nedd Fechan to   ₋tradfellte road, there is a gated
track opposite the turning to Porth-yr-Ogof. This tarmac track bears right towards
the farm but a rough track straight ahead leads onto the moor. At a point where
an obscure track leads off left from this track, by a hawthorn tree, head roughly
northwest to a very large, shallow depression. The entrance to the cave is at the
bottom of this depression, near an old stone wall, and sometimes takes water.
Description   Although of short length, this cave is an important speleological site
and the water has been tested to a resurgence in the Mellte opposite the Paul
Esser bench at Porth-yr-Ogof.
The entrance is a small slot which leads to a series of tight squeezes and small
chambers.
History   First explored by HCC in 1952.

Town Drain Grade 3
Alternative name: Arcade Cave

Grid Ref SN 9110 1367   OS Maps 1:50 000 sheet 160,
1:25 000   Brecon Beacons Central O/L

Altitude : 288 metres

Length : 494 metres

Location   The entrance(s) is in the bank of the Nedd Fechan and can be
reached by following the river downstream (usually dry in summer) from Bridge
Cave, past Cwm-Pwll-y-Rhyd, to the resurgence of White Lady Cave. Town Drain
is a few metres beyond White Lady in the opposite bank under an overhanging
cliff.

Description   Despite its name, this cave is quite interesting and the first section
is very pleasant. It does however, get quite muddy towards its end.
The main entrance is a walk-in size slot which leads to a passage coming from a
smaller entrance to the left. Turning right, the passage makes a couple of right-
angled turns to a straight section with clean scalloped walls. Beyond this the roof
soon lowers and the walls and floor are often coated in a this layer of mud from
floodwater. Progress continues by crawling, stooping, and walking, through a
series of right-angled bends to a point where a small stream enters from the right.
Downstream, the passage then descends in a lofty rift and, just after a short drop
into a pool, another inlet passage enters on the left. *This inlet passage can be
followed for some way via some squeezes and a crawl in water.*
Continuing downstream from the inlet, the main passage meanders and gradually
decreases in size until it becomes choked with mud and stones. There are a few
short high-level passages but unfortunately they lead nowhere.

History   First explored by T.Braithwaite in 1936. Survey by UBSS in 1970.
WARNING : THE CAVE IS LIABLE TO FLOOD.

White Lady Cave Grade 2

Grid Ref SN9111 1368   OS Maps 1:50 000 sheet 160,
1:25 000 Brecon Beacons Central O/L

Altitude : 288 metres

Length : 300 metres + (inc.Cwm Pwll-y-Rhyd)

Location   Follow the old river bed beyond Cwm Pwll-y-Rhyd until a climb down
brings you back to present river course. The river resurges from the cave which is
on the right.

Description   A nice cave but rather short as most of its length is beyond a long
sump (see Cwm Pwll-y-Rhyd).
The large entrance gives access to a large, highly scalloped, oval-shaped river
passage with several deep pools. The easiest route is along the right-hand wall
where it is possible to avoid getting wet above the thighs. About 15 m in, a very
deep pool may be avoided by going through an eyehole squeeze in the right-
hand wall. Beyond this the river becomes shallower and the passage more lofty
before ending at a large sump pool.

THE SUMP IS 27 M LONG AND ONLY PASSABLE TO DIVERS AND CONNECTS WITH CWM PWLL-Y-RHYD. PART WAY ALONG THIS SUMP A BRANCH SUMP LEADS TO WHITE LADY 2 AFTER A DIVE OF 70 M. THERE IS SOME 245 M OF OPEN PASSAGE BEYOND WHICH IS SOMETIMES ACCESSIBLE FROM CWM PWLL-Y-RHYD WITHOUT DIVING EQUIPMENT. *Back in the main passage, looking towards the entrance, there are two small high level passages on the left.* Another larger passage on the right contains some nice gours and a few other decorations before reaching a deep pool and a duck. Beyond the duck is a second entrance which is situated immediately to one side of the main entrance. *There is also a crawl on the left which connects with the main river passage.*

History   First recorded exploration was by T.Braithwaite in 1936. Underwater connection with Cwm Pwll-y-Rhyd proved by CDG in 1960.

WARNING : THE CAVE IS LIABLE TO FLOOD.

Y Gwal

Grade 1

Grid Ref SN9205 1400 OS Maps 1:50 000 sheet 160, 1:25 000 Brecon Beacons Central O/L	

Altitude : 350 metres

Length : 30 metres

Location   Situated on the moor to the north of the Hole By The Wall. It is surrounded by a fence.

Description   The entrance is a collapse and an awkward climb leads to a muddy boulder slope which descends to a large keyhole-shaped passage. This impressive passage is not many metres below the surface and is unfortunately completely blocked at the far end by a muddy boulder choke. Near the entrance a short crawl leads to a small passage ending in boulders, again near the surface of the moor.

Tackle   A 15 m rope is useful for the entrance climb.

History   The cave was first explored and surveyed by B.Kenny and A.Jones.

Lesser Caves and Sites of Speleological Interest

Badger Hole   SN9117 1392
Berthlwyd Boundary Swallet   SN9124 1293
Berthlwyd Road Swallet   SN9132 1326
Berthlwyd Swallet   SN9132 1315
Blaen Nedd Urchaf Resurgence   SN9056 1540
Blaen Nedd Urchaf Sink   SN9033 1549
Blaen Nedd Urchaf Swallet   SN9043 1550
Buttertubs Cave   SN941 128
Carn-y-Botel Pot   SN9557 1439
Cwm Huw Bwub   SN910 128
Einon's Hole   SN9160 1420
Cwm Porth Farm Well   SN9194 1212
Green Cave   SN9410 1263
Gulping Holes   SN925 128

Gwaen Cefn-y-Garreg Rock Shelter   SN9433 1338
Gwaen Cefn-y-Garreg Sink   SN9408 1297
Lesser Pulpit Hole   SN9407 1290
Lewis's Pot   SN9040 1552
Lewis's Quarry Pots   SN9536 1150
Little Badger Cave   SN9116 1394
Little Neath River Cave Resurgence   SN9119 1207
Little White Lady Cave   SN9113 1375
Maes y Gawnen Pots   SN906 141
Mellte Main Sink   SN9315 1332
Obvious Cave   SN9223 1350
Ogofau Gwynion   SN921 145
Ogof Berthlwyd   SN9156 1274
Ogof Cadno   SN9117 1241
Ogof Cagoule   SN9120 1208
Ogof Carnau Gwynion Caves   SN9173 1485
Ogof Clarwydden   SN911 125
Ogof Cwbl Hardd   SN9119 1228
Ogof Dau Gi   SN923 125
Ogof Ffynnon Fach   SN9340 1201
Ogof Ffynnon Sink   SN936 122
Ogof Ganol   SN9329 1216
Ogof Gwynion No.1   SN9221 1461
Ogof Gwynion No.2   SN9209 1458
Ogof Gwynion West Digs   SN9200 1458
Ogof Lliwiog   SN9155 1275
Ogof Nantes   SN9118 1417
Ogof Plas y Daren   SN9206 1236
Ogof Siom   SN9116 1239
Ogof Siom Bach   SN950 135
Ogof y Daren   SN9203 1239
Pant Mawr Rising   SN9120 1227
Pant y Llwyn Farm Resurgence   SN9216 1229
Pant y Llwyn Fissures   SN9211 1238
Plas y Daren Cave   SN9228 1271
Plas y Daren Fissures   SN9202 1238
Plas y Daren Pot   SN9229 1263
Plas y Daren Potholes   SN9207 1236
Productus Pot   SN9025 1402
Pwll Derw Sink   SN9413 1235
Pwll Derwen   SN9095 1310
Pwll Du   SN9121 1206
Pwll y Felin Sink   SN9420 1207
Pwll y Ffordd Cave   SN9154 1267
Pwll y Gelynen Sink   SN9185 1282
Rhododendron Pot   SN9237 1289
Theoretical Pot   SN9162 1476

Town Drain photo. by Tim Stratford

7. Swansea Valley

Craig-y-Nos Quarry Cave

Grade 2

Grid Ref SN8420 1500   OS Maps 1:50 000 sheet 160,
1:25 000 Beacons Western O/L

Altitude: 274 metres

Length: 305 metres

Location   From Craig-y-Nos Hospital on the main road from Sennybridge to Swansea climb over the gate which is a few metres down the road on the right-hand side. Follow the old mineral track to the remains of some old quarry buildings and then start to climb up the shoulder between two quarries. The entrance to the cave is at the top of the shoulder about halfway up the face.
Description   An easy cave of mainly small passages which is ideal for beginners. The entrance crawl very quickly leads into a walking size passage and a junction. *To the right the passage leads for a short distance to end in several very small sandy passages.* To the left the main passage descends quite steeply to end abruptly at two sandy crawls which quickly close down. A few metres before this on the left-hand side, two passages, one a tight sandy tube, the other a bedding plane crawl, lead into a small chamber. From here a descending passage leads to a junction, turn right and the passage continues to descend. After some way a squeeze is encountered and soon after this the passage becomes completely choked with mud. There are a few side passages but all are choked within a few feet.
History   Surveyed by S.W.C.C. in 1953.

Cwm Dwr Quarry Cave 2

Grade 3

Grid Ref SN8572 1562   OS Maps 1:50 000 sheet 160,
1:25 000 Brecon Beacons Western O/L

Length: 370 metres approx.

Location   Situated in the same quarry as the Cwm Dwr entrance to Ogof Ffynnon Ddu.
Description   A small cave which is probably part of the Ffynnon Ddu system but is, as yet, unconnected.
A 5m deep entrance shaft leads to a sizeable passage which is followed to a sump which needs to be pumped. Beyond the sump, the small passage leads to a junction with a small stream. Upstream is Ping Pong Passage which ends in boulders.   Downstream after a short distance is a 13m pitch into a chamber, Default Chamber. At one end is a boulder slope leading to a sand filled passage and at the other end the streamway continues. The streamway can be followed for about 200 m before ending at a sump.
History   The cave was first discovered in 1938. Re-discovered in 1990 and extended by SWCC. Survey SWCC Newsletter 109 1991.

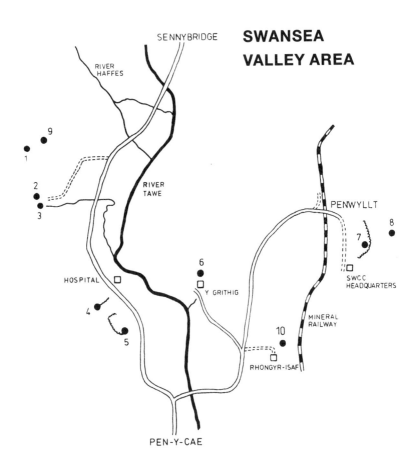

SWANSEA VALLEY AREA

1. PWLL DWFN
2. OGOF-YR-ESGYRN
3. DAN-YR-OGOF
4. HOSPITAL CAVE
5. CRAIG-Y-NOS QUARRY CAVE
6. OGOF FFYNNON DDU 1
7. CWM DWR QUARRY CAVE
8. OGOF FFYNNON DD 2
9. TUNNEL CAVE
10. OGOF-YR-ARDD

Dan Yr Ogof

Grade 3/5

Grid Ref SN8382 1600   OS Maps 1:50 000 sheet 160,
1:25 000 Brecon Beacons Western O/L

Altitude: 216 metres

Length: 15,500 metres

Location   Situated on the western side of the Swansea Valley. Just past the hospital at Craig-y-Nos a tarmac drive on the left leads to a car park by the cave. The first part of the cave is open to the public and so it is well signposted.
Access   Access to Dan-yr-Ogof is to be administered by a Cave Management Committee. Details have yet to be worked out but meantime contact the Secretary SWCC for access. A leadership scheme is in operation.
Description   This is one of the major Welsh systems and provides a sporting trip with many interesting features and plenty of fine formations.
The first part of the cave is a show cave with concrete paths and steps. Cavers are asked to pass through this part of the cave quietly, causing as little inconvenience to the tourists as possible. The show cave is a series of phreatic type passages and chambers, with some fine formations, ending at Bridge Chamber.

Dan-Yr-Ogof 1 (1937 series)

Grade 3

From Bridge Chamber, beyond the railings, a flight of concrete steps leads directly to Lake 1. This is now passed by a concrete path on the left-hand side to a sand bank. The passage leads directly to Lake 2, normally quite shallow, and is followed by a small sand bank to Lake 3. This is a much longer and deeper lake and leads to the Cataracts and two short pools. *To the left, two small passages lead to the sump into Syphon Series.* Straight on is Lake 4 which is short but quite deep.
At the far side of Lake 4, a climb-up on the right leads to a rift passage. After a few metres it is necessary to climb up again, by a large boulder, into a higher section of the passage which leads after a short distance to a larger sandy passage opposite a fine array of formations. *To the right is a 6m drop to Pot Sump which connects with Lake 3.* To the left the passage is followed to a boulder slope, at the top of which is a climb-up into the Boulder Chamber. *By climbing up on the right-hand wall it is also possible to gain access to a small passage leading to Wigmore Hall.* An easier route avoiding the climb is made by following a crawl straight ahead from the top of the boulder slope into a small chamber, then an easy climb into a passage on the right followed by a left turn to emerge from boulders in the floor of the Boulder Chamber. *A scree slope on the left-hand side of this large chamber leads to the Mud Chamber and the high level August Series.* The way on is at the end of the chamber by turning right into a small passage which leads to Straw chamber. *To the right are some fine straws and formations, and the way into Corbel's Chamber.* To the left the chamber is low and leads to a crawl over boulders until the roof rises *and a short climb gives access to Shower Aven and the start of the very tight and tortuous Longer Crawl which leads into Dan-yr-Ogof 2. This is not the normal route and can only be followed by persons of small build.*

The normal route is via the Long Crawl and is straight ahead from Shower Aven. The passage beyond the aven gradually becomes smaller until it meets the Cattle Trough at the start of the Long Crawl. Turn left along the trough which usually has some water in it and follow the passage to a sharp left turn into a narrow rift. A climb up through a hole in the roof then leads to a higher level passage which then slopes down to an awkward right-angled bend which is stony and tight. The crawl continues over stony and calcite floors for about 45m and is quite tight in places. At the end a slippery climb down through a hole on the left leads to the head of the pitch into Gerrard Platten Hall. A 6m fixed chain ladder is used for the descent and care must be taken when getting on and off the ladder at the top of the pitch.

Dan-Yr-Ogof 2 (1966 Series)   Grade 4

A small stream flows across the floor of Gerrard Platten Hall. To the right (upstream) soon ends in a large boulder choke but the way on is to the left. After about 35m the stream disappears down a large hole marking the entrance to the Lower Series. By continuing across the top of the hole a large crystal pool is reached. *Straight ahead is Flabbergasm Oxbow, finely decorated, which leads after about 90m to a 7m overhanging descent into the Grand Canyon. Entry to Flabbergasm should be made by traversing around the left-hand side of the crystal pool.* The normal way on is to the left of the crystal pool into a large sandy passage which is the start of the Grand Canyon. After a few metres it becomes a very high and impressive keyhole shaped passage with some fine forests of helictites on the right-hand wall. The roof eventually lowers and the canyon enters a wide sandy passage with some fine straws where care must be taken to avoid damage with your head. The roof soon becomes even lower and some candle-grease formations are reached. To the left of these formations a climb up a mud slope leads into the very large Monk Hall. *On the left as you enter the hall are two passages which soon become blocked by boulders but the nearer of the two gives access to the Longer Crawl which goes back to Dan-yr-Ogof 1.* Continuing to the right, Monk Hall leads to Cloud Chamber with its magnificent 'clouds, of straws, some of which are up to 5m long. *A small stream flows along the chamber and disappears into Four Pots Passage, a tortuous connection with the Lower Series.* The chamber quickly decreases in size and enters Cascade Aven with its waterfall to the right. Straight ahead a tricky climb leads directly to the Green Canal. *To the left at the start of the Canal is a hole going up into the large Hanger Passage which ends in a large boulder choke. A way through the choke on the left hand side leads to two further large passages, Hanger South and Hanger North.* The Green Canal starts narrow and deep and necessitates a swim. After quite a long distance the Canal becomes wider and shallower enabling the last part to be waded. A short distance beyond the end of the Canal the passage opens into the side of the large Trench Way. To the left the passage passes Avalanche Corner and then the floor suddenly falls away into a large black space – The Abyss – leading via a chimney climb to the Lower Series. To the right leads to Go Faster Passage which starts out quite high but gradually becomes lower and wider. A fork is reached and *to the left the passage leads over sand banks to Surprise Chamber* but the way on is to the right through a narrow slot. This is Go Slower Passage and after about 75m enters the large Rottenstone Aven with its boulder floor. The passage continues beyond *and there are several entrances on the right to the narrow Tunnel Two Passage.* A short wet section follows leading out into the very large Bat Chamber. The passage from Bat Chamber is large and goes through three wide bends to where the stream is met sinking between boulders. *On the right at the last bend is Bog Passage* while upstream the passage continues high and wide to The Rising and the climb-up leading to Dan-yr-Ogof 3.

Lower Series   Grade 4

From Gerrard Platten Hall a climb down leads to a sandy passage which bears to the left. The passage is followed to an awkward climb down into a small chamber. *Straight ahead there are several ways down to a sump* but the way on is to the right along a stooping height passage to another chamber. Climb up on the ledge to the right leads to Virgin Passage with its gours and deep pools. Virgin Passage is followed for some distance to a sandy climb down to The Washing Machine, a noisy spout of water falling into a deep pool. Cross the rock bridge between the Washing Machine and a deep pool and then a climb up on the right leads to a phreatic tube and then to a small chamber. To the right is the start of Bakerloo Straight, a fine large phreatic tube which ends after about 150m at Lake 10. A climb-up on the left just before Lake 10 leads to a stooping height passage and then to a small chamber. *To the left is a climb down through boulders to the Mazeways* while to the right leads under a water spout to Thixotropic Passage. The passage is followed for some distance to the Camel's Back, a steep climb-up over a narrow slot, and then to the Abyss. At the far end of this very large chamber is an awkward chimney climb to Trench Way. *To the left of this climb is a difficult rift climb which leads to Dali's Delight and Tubeways.*

Dan-Yr-Ogof 3   Grade 5

At the Rising a climb up a fixed chain ladder leads to a free climb up a rift (the centre route is now worn and slippery) for about 10m. This is then followed by an awkward move to gain access to a window in the opposite overhanging wall. This is Windy Way, a 40m hands and knees crawl which leads to the top of an awkward climb down to the start of Birthday Passage traverse. This is a 45 degree traverse over several deep lakes to a sandy floored rift with fine helictites. A short squeeze under a fallen block leads to a small chamber at the head of the Great North Road pitch. A rawbolt is in position and a ladder is required. An awkward take off opens to a fine free hanging pitch which lands on the floor of the Great North Road.

Downstream a sump is met but upstream a wide river passage is followed to the first of many boulder falls. After about 450m the stream issues from a slot on the left and the best way on is via a ledge on the right-hand wall. The route ascends and crosses the river passage, some 10m or so above the stream, by means of a fallen block. A larger ledge is then followed to a short climb-down which leads to the highest point of Pinnacle Chamber. the chamber ahead opens out to over 9m wide and 18m high with the Pinnacle, a large detached rock flake, visible at the far end of the chamber. *Two avens in the right-hand wall lead to the high level Pinnacle Series and some fine formations.* Beyond the Pinnacle the North

Bypass is entered and there is a choice of two ways on. A climb down through boulders leads to the Meanders and the stream, while a climb up through boulders straight ahead leads via a sharp left bend and a sloping ledge back into the Meanders. A short way on, a 3m climb up on the right-hand wall leads to the Mostest with its fine crystal floor. The stream can be followed to a large chamber full of sand banks and strewn with large boulders. At the far end of the chamber the passage ends in a sand choke but this is bypassed by climbing the North Aven which is about 30m back down the passage on the right-hand wall. *At the base of the aven is a low passage which leads to the Mostest* while two short climbs, a traverse, and a chimney type climb with the best holds on the right-hand wall leads to Overpass Passage at the top. A boulder slope then leads to the top of a large chamber nearly filled with sand. The way on is down to the left where the stream is rejoined. A short traverse over the stream and through a narrow slot leads into the Starting Gate. Two streams meet here. *To the right a large passage soon closes down and leads to the Right-Hand Series which ends after about 400m at grit choked avens.* To the left of the Starting Gate is the Left-Hand Series of much larger dimensions. After passing under several large avens the passage takes on an almost square shape with a flat roof. The passage turns sharp left and passes several large grit boulders under the Gritstone Avens. The passage ahead becomes larger and enters the Dunes (sand cliffs) and then into the Grand Hall some 12m wide and 12m high. At the far end of the chamber is a huge boulder choke, the Far North Choke. This effectively marks the end of the cave although some small passages have been explored here in an attempt to pass the choke, so far without great success.

Tackle   Great North Road Pitch – 15m ladder and lifeline.
A wet suit is essential for crossing the lakes.

History   The cave was first explored by the Morgan brothers in 1912. Major extensions made by the 'Dragon Group' in 1937 and by members of the S.W.C.C. and C.D.G. from 1964 to the present day.
Survey – BCRA Transactions Vol. 4 Nos. 1/2 March 1977.

Downey's Cave   Grade 2

Grid Ref SN8485 1546   OS Maps 1:50 000 sheet 160,
                                          1:25 000 Brecon Beacons Western O/L

Altitude: 221 metres

Length: 61 metres

Location   The entrance to the cave is situated in a wooded slope above Ogof Ffynnon Ddu.
Description   A small cave of low and narrow passages which is really part of the Ffynnon Ddu system with which it connects.
History   First explored by the S.W.C.C. in 1946.
Survey included on the Ogof Ffynnon Ddu survey by S.W.C.C. in 1969.

Hospital Cave   Grade 2
Alternative name: Waterfall Cave

Grid Ref SN8394 1722   OS Maps 1:50 000 sheet 160,
                                        1:25 000 Brecon Beacons Western O/L

Altitude: 274 metres

Length: 220 metres approx.

Location   The entrance to the cave is situated on the side of Cribarth opposite
Craig-y-Nos Hospital. In wet weather the water resurging from the cave can be
seen from the road as it pours over the edge of the dam which has been built in
front of the cave.
Description   Only the first 120m of the cave can be explored by ordinary cavers,
the rest being only accessible to divers.
A climb over the inner wall of the dam leads to the streamway and a crawl
through a low arch which becomes a duck in wet weather. Beyond the arch there
are two ways on. One route follows the water upstream through mainly small
passage to a squeeze into a small chamber while a much larger dry passage on
the left leads to a crawl into the same chamber. A climb up through loose
boulders then leads to a larger chamber followed by a low phreatic passage. A
sandy crawl then leads to a sump. There are several high level passages all of
which are small and close down after a short distance.
**THE SUMP HAS BEEN PASSED BY DIVERS TO MORE SUMPS WITH ONLY SMALL
AMOUNTS OF PASSAGE BETWEEN THEM. THE FIRST SUMP IS 15M LONG FOLLOWED
BY SUMPS OF 6M, 27M, 9M, 3M, 3M, 3M, AND 9M. THE LIMIT OF EXPLORATION AT
PRESENT IS SUMP 9 WHICH HAS BEEN DIVED FOR 6M.**
Tackle   A wet suit is advisable in wet weather.
History   Being an active resurgence the cave has probably been known for a
long time.

Ogof Ffynnon Ddu   Grade 2/5

Grid Ref SN 8480 1530 (OFD 1) SN8575 1560 (Cwm Dwr) SN 8635 1589
(Top Entrance)   OS Maps 1:50 000 sheet 160,
                                        1:25 000 Brecon Beacons Western O/L

Altitude: 204 metres OFD 1   432 metres Top Entrance

Length: 50,000 metres approx.

Vertcal Range : 308 metres

Location   Just to the north of Pen-y-Cae on the Swansea to Sennybridge road
(A4067) a turning leads to a small road going up the hill to Penwyllt and the
S.W.C.C. Headquarters. There are three entrances to OFD, the first being the
entrance to OFD 1 which is at the bottom of the hill behind Y Grithig farm. The
second way of entry is via Cwm Dwr Quarry Cave which is situated in the quarry
next to the S.W.C.C. Headquarters and the third entrance (Top Entrance) is
situated on the hillside behind the S.W.C.C.
Access   The cave is a Nature Reserve and access is controlled by a Cave
management Committee. A permit is required for entry and this should be applied
for well in advance by writing to Permit Secretary, S.W.C.C. Headquarters, Powell

Street, Penwyllt, Pen-y-Cae, Nr. Swansea. Access is only to bone-fide caving clubs. Parties wishing to enter via the OFD 1 entrance must have a leader who is a recognised leader for that system.

Description   Ogof Ffynnon Ddu is the deepest cave in Britain and the second longest, and ranks amongst the longest caves in the world. The cave comprises of a complex system of large and small fossil passages, finely decorated in places, and a fine and very long streamway. The cave is divided into four distinct sections – OFD 1, Cwm Dwr, OFD 2, and OFD 3. Through trips between the entrances are possible but should not be attempted without a reasonable knowledge of the cave from both ends as it is easy to get lost.

Due to its length and complexity it is impossible to give a complete description of the cave in the space available in this book. Therefore only the main routes are described with brief details of the many series which lead off from these.

Ogof Ffynnon Ddu 1   /ๅๅ๒   Grade 4

The entrance shaft is descended via three fixed iron ladders to the upper end of Gothic passage. The passage is followed along a well trodden route *and passes the entrance to Skeleton Chamber, with its connection to Downey's Cave, on the left.* There are several small passages on the right but the main passage goes through several bends, past a formation known as The Font, to the foot of a fixed steel ladder which leads up to the *Toast Rack on the left*. Straight ahead is a pool, Pluto's Bath, which leads to a descending passage and the Main Streamway. Downstream the water enters a system of bedding planes before ending in the sump that leads to the resurgence. Upstream the Main Streamway twists and turns for about 600m and there are some deep steep sections which become very sporty in high water conditions. There are four deep pots across which have been laid some pipes to aid progress. Care should be taken in high water as these are difficult to spot and a fall into one of the pots could prove fatal. At the far end of the Main Streamway most of the water issues from a sump on the right and a small stream enters from a lofty passage which continues to the left. This passage is followed past the way into the *Railton-Wild Series on the left and then the chain on the climb up to Lowe's Passage* to a cascaded which falls from the Waterfall Series above. Straight on the passage leads to Boulder Chamber with its large collapse of boulders through which a route along the right-hand wall leads to Hush Sump, Dip Sump, and the connection to Cwmdwr and OFD 2.

The easiest way into the Waterfall Series is via a fairly easy climb at the cascade, which leads to a large dry passage. Straight ahead under a large boulder leads into a stream passage. After a short distance a climb up a sandy slope on the left leads to a large dry passage – The Dry Way – while straight ahead with the stream is the smaller Wet Way. Following the Dry Way leads into a chamber from which there are two ways on. *Straight ahead a climb up a fixed chain leads to a series of passages called the West Leg* while to the right a short sandy passage leads to a junction. To the right is the Wet Way while to the left, following a small stream upstream, leads to a small chamber. Here most of the water enters from the left and can be followed upstream to the East Leg which connects with the West Leg via Cross Passage. *To the right of the chamber a climb up a calcited waterfall leads to a small passage with some fine helictites and then a rift climb leads to the large Crystal Pool Chamber with its fine pool at the far end. From*

here two passages to the right lead to climbs down into the Canyon.
Back in the Streamway a climb up the chain into Lowe's Passage leads to the
large Upper Series and the escape route used in the case of sudden flooding. At
the far end of Lowe's Passage a climb up through boulders leads to the large
Rawl Series. To the left is the large flat roofed Starlight Chamber while to the right
a series of large boulder and sandy floored passages lead to Pi Chamber and
Pillar Chamber. A route down through boulders then leads to a traverse high
above the Main Streamway. The more difficult parts of this long traverse are aided
by fixed wire handlines. The route passes through a series of small passages
above stream level to the Toast Rack and then a climb down the fixed steel
ladder leads back into the Entrance Series.

Cwmdwr Quarry Cave   Grade 4

The entrance shaft begins with a section of concrete drainpipe and then down
over shoring timbers to a chamber at the bottom. The way on is to the left and
then to the right, through a low opening which takes a small stream. The stream
is followed bearing left at fork, along a crawl to a T junction. Turning right leads to
a section of dry sandy crawls called Dim Dwr which if followed for some distance
to a tighter section where a small stream appears. Soon after the stream is met
and beyond a shallow pool, a climb through boulders leads into the Jama, a
spacious passage with a sandy floor. To the right ends in a boulder choke while
to the left a climb down over boulders leads to a stream which crosses at right-
angles. *Downstream it quickly sumps and upstream ends in a boulder choke.*
By crossing over the stream and climbing up on the other side leads to a lofty
stream passage which is followed to another larger, stream. Turning left, following
the stream *past a sandy passage which leads to Dripping Aven*, the lofty
passage ends in a huge boulder choke. The way through the choke starts low
down on the right and a well worn route goes up and over through boulders and
finishes in a sandy crawl.
On the other side of the choke are the Big Shacks, large boulder chambers which
lead to a complex series of passages. The main route on is through a short
narrow passage on the right and then left along a well trod sandy floored
passage. This leads to a high level route along a narrow rift passage and involves
some short traverses. At the far end of the passage a short climb down leads to
a junction with a large sandy passage. To the left the passage leads to a series of
passages heading back towards the Big Shacks while to the right the passage
slopes down to the Smithy. A large hole in the floor of the Smithy leads to a climb
down through boulders into the Cwmdwr Stream. The stream passage, which is
narrow, is followed to a dry bypass at the end of which a climb down back into
the stream leads to The Confluence where the Main Ffynnon Ddu stream is met.
The alternative Dry Route leads off at the left-hand (eastern) end of the Smithy
and bears round right to the junction with The Nether Rawl. To the right leads to a
series of passages, one of which leads back to the Smithy while another leads to
the Big Shacks. The Dry Route continues to the left along the Nether Rawl to a
large chamber known as Piccadilly. Here, several passages converge. To the left
leads via Flood Bypass to the confluence while to the right the passage ascends
to end in a scree run-in covered in a soft white deposit – Heol Eira. Two other
routes straight ahead lead to the Dip Sump Series and the connection with Ogof
Ffynnon Ddu 1.

Ogof Ffynnon Ddu 2   lo mAy 199)   Grade 2/4

The part of the cave known as Ffynnon Ddu II is the largest and most complex part of the cave. It is easy to get lost if you are unfamiliar with the main routes. It is probably best tackled using a combination of this guide book and a copy of the survey which is usually available from the SWCC Headquarters.

The Top Entrance leads via a steep slope into a large dry passage. *Near the bottom of the slope, in the lefthand wall, is a small hole which enters an aven which can be free-climbed to a passage leading to the Mini Columns and then via a wet, muddy crawl to the White Arch Series. A small hole low down on the right-hand side of the entrance passage also leads via a crawl to the White Arch Series, while two large passages on the left lead to the very large and aptly named Big Chamber Near the Entrance. From here a series of passages on the left leads to the pitch into Column Hall with its fine calcite pillars, while to the right of the Big Chamber a passage leads to the Labyrinth, Bagpipe Chamber, and the upper level of Arete Chamber.*

Continuing to the far end of the entrance passage, *the more normal route into White Arch Series is to the right* while to the left the passage becomes smaller over slippery boulders and leads to the Brickyard. A climb up over a large boulder on the left and then a clamber over more large boulders leads to a narrow passage. Turn right into a sandy passage and on into a small chamber. *A large passage on the right is another way into White Arch Series and by following it for a short distance and taking the first passage to the right is an alternative route back to the Brickyard. A small passage to the left of the small chamber leads to the upper levels of Arete Chamber and the Labyrinth* but the main way on is straight ahead along a winding sandy passage to Gnome Passage. Gnome Passage is a large square-shaped passage with many small stalagmites growing on the boulder floor. A path has been taped through the formations and this should be strictly followed. *About halfway along the passage a hole at the base of the left-hand wall leads to Edwards Shortcut, a route eventually ending at Selenite Tunnel.* Gnome Passage ends at a large boulder choke and just before this *a passage on the right leads back to the White Arch Series and the entrance.* At the near end of Gnome Passage a sandy boulder slope on the left leads to the Wedding Cake and then the large Chasm Passage. Straight ahead is The Shakehole, a deep pit which spans the width of the passage, while to the left is a descending boulder slope.

At the bottom of the boulder slope it is possible to squeeze down through the boulders on the right-hand side (take CARE!) into a narrow descending rift and then to a junction with Salubrious Passage which carries a small stream. *Upstream leads to the bottom of Arete Chamber* while downstream, to the left, the passage is high and narrow and continues for some considerable distance, via a short climb down, to a point where the passage takes a sharp right-handed turn. *An obvious dry passage straight ahead leads to The Trident and The Judge, two very large calcite formations. The passage beyond the Judge leads over the inlet stream of Swamp Creek to the pitch into The Nave followed by another pitch into Pendulum Passage (NOTE: a trip to or from the Crevasse along Pendulum Passage requires an exchange trip between two parties as there are pitches down into Pendulum from both ends.)* Continuing down Salubrious Passage over boulders covered in an unusual white mud leads to a squeeze past a large boulder into The Crossroads. *To the right a narrow*

NYTH BRAN SERIES

A small part of the complex system of Ogof Ffynnon Ddu

0 10 60
metres

N

Creek Alley

Nant Bach

Chasm Passage

NYTH BRAN SERIES

based on survey by S.S.S.

passage leads to Selenite Tunnel and Edwards Shortcut while a step-up into a passage on the left-hand wall leads to a step over Maypole Inlet. *The passage on the other side of the Inlet leads to the Cross Rift and then to a chamber at the end of Midnight Passage. To the right of the chamber leads into a series of passages leading to Northern Lights and the northern part of the Upper Great Oxbow Series. To the left of the chamber is Midnight Passage itself which leads to a traverse into the Upper Great Oxbow Series and a high level route above the Mainstream.*

A few metres beyond the step over Maypole Inlet a short passage on the left leads to a climb down through jammed boulders to the inlet stream. Following the inlet downstream the passage is high but very narrow and meandering and leads to a fixed ladder climb down. Below the ladder an awkward climb then leads down into the Main Stream Passage. The Main Stream Passage is over 3000m long and can be followed upstream, via the Second Oxbow and some fine cascades to end at a spectacular 8m high waterfall known as Top Waterfall. Downstream the passage descends gently to a sump which is bypassed by a climb up into the Great Oxbow. After some distance the stream is rejoined and followed to the Marble Showers where the marbling effect of calcite bands through the black limestone is very striking. *Here, an easy 8m climb leads to the Marble Showers Series.* Continuing down the mainstream leads to the First River Chamber just before which *a small passage on the right leads via a difficult climb to Fault Aven Series.* Beyond the First River Chamber the stream continues to a low arch and The Confluence, where the Cwm Dwr stream enters from the right. (NOTE: The Main Stream Passage is in fact best tackled by going upstream, against the flow i.e. the through trip between OFD 2 and Cwm Dwr is best done from Cwm Dwr to OFD 2, especially if the water is high. In the event of flooding there are markers to indicate safe places to exit the streamway.)

Following Salubrious Passage upstream leads to the bottom of Arete Chamber. *To the left is a narrow meandering passage which leads to the Labyrinth and then Cairn Chamber from where a climb up leads to a route back to the Big Chamber Near The Entrance. A climb up on the right-hand wall beside flowstone leads to a small passage which ends at the top of a slippery climb down (rope advisable) to the boulder slope in Chasm Passage.* The main way on is straight ahead in the continuation of Salubrious which ends at a choke. Just before the choke, two small passages on the right lead to a narrow meandering crawl. The crawl emerges into a large passage, effectively the further end of Chasm Passage. To the left leads to a choke while to the right leads to a sharp right-handed bend. *Part way along, on the left, is a small passage which leads to part of the Nyth Bran Series and the obscure route into Prokofiev Series. Also on the left, at the right hand bend, is a climb up to an ascending passage leading to the higher levels of Nyth Bran.* Continuing along Chasm Passage, a steep slope leads to a junction with a sizeable passage on the left. *Straight ahead is the far side of The Shakehole* while following the passage to the left leads to the Poached Egg Climb, an awkward climb down which is tackled on the right-hand side. The sandy floored passage at the bottom of the climb is followed to a junction chamber, Bhowani Junction. *To the right, an awkward wet climb leads to a small ascending passage which joins a high level passage running from Nyth Bran to high above the floor in Chasm Passage. To the left is Straw Gallery and another passage leading to the Nyth Bran Series.* Continuing along the main passage via an easy climb down leads past the entrance to the Nant Gam stream, on the right, to another junction. *High passage on the left is Creek Alley, yet another way into the Nyth Bran Series,* while continuing down through boulders on the right the main passage eventually reaches The Crevasse. *The Crevasse can be descended by ladder or rope to reach Pendulum Passage* but a traverse over the top leads to a pitch from jammed boulders which can be free-climbed but is best tackled with an 8m ladder or rope. From the bottom of the pitch, a large boulder pile is ascended to a chamber. Bearing left leads to a chimney climb below a large boulder into a narrow passage. The passage is followed to a difficult climb up of 3m and then to an area of shattered limestone - The Shambles. Climb up on the left, with care, and down on the other side. Another short climb up then leads to the Traverses. The first traverse is a tricky ledge on the left-hand wall (there is a useful finger hold half-way along). The following traverses are fairly straight forward with narrow ledges on both walls, except for the last one which starts off wide, with a ledge on the right wall, but narrows to become easier. Beyond the final traverse, a boulder pile leads to a boulder choke and a squeeze, on the left, into Ffynnon Ddu III."

Ogof Ffynnon Ddu 3 Grade 5

Beyond the boulder choke the main Ffynnon Ddu stream is met in a chamber. Downstream the water can be followed for over 200m until it ends in a sump, the water re-emerging in OFD 2 at the Top Waterfall. Upstream, progress is barred by two waterfalls which can only be passed in very low water conditions. The normal route on is via a maypole bridge into a high level passage which is followed for some distance bypassing the waterfalls. The stream is rejoined at an obvious sloping shelf and is followed through wide meandering passage for a considerable distance. *At several places along the streamway it is possible to climb up into a series of high level passages.* At the far end of the streamway a low canal, which sumps in high water conditions, leads to a large boulder floored chamber – Smith's Armoury. The stream rises from the boulders and marks the end of the cave.

Tackle   Many of the fixed aids throughout the cave have now been removed and it is best to check the list in the SWCC Headquarters before entering the cave.

   The Nave – 12m ladder, belay and lifeline
   The Crevasse – 23m ladder, long belay and lifeline
   Pitch beyond The Crevasse – 8m ladder, belay and lifeline
   Pendulum Passage –   9m ladder or rope, belay and lifeline
                        6m ladder or rope, belay and lifeline
                        12m ladder or rope, belay and lifeline
                        6m ladder or rope, belay and lifeline
                        (needs to be laddered from both directions)
   Column Hall – 18m ladder or rope, belay and lifeline
   Cwm Dwr Entrance – 8m ladder or rope, and belay

History   OFD 1 was first explored by members of the S.W.C.C. in 1946 after digging operations. OFD 2 discovered by divers in 1966. Major extensions, connection with Cwm Dwr, and OFD 3 discovered in 1966.
Survey by S.W.C.C. in 1969.
Nyth Bryn Series resurveyed by S.S.S. in 1984.
WARNING   The stream passages are liable to flood. The OFD 2 streamway is long and can be very strenuous in high water and should only be attempted by very experienced cavers in these conditions.

Ogof Pant Canol   Grade 2

Grid Ref SN8492 1536   OS Maps: 1:50 000 sheet 160,
                                                 1:25 000 Brecon Beacons Western O/L

Altitude: 244 metres

Length: 76 metres

Location   The entrance is situated in a small cliff above the entrance to Ogof
Ffynnon Ddu 1.
Description   A small cave which involves a very tight squeeze and an
underground lake which is really part of the Ffynnon Ddu system with which it
connects.
History   The cave was first explored by E. J. Mason in 1942.

Ogof-yr-Ardd   Grade 4
Alternative names : Pen Blwydd yr Ogof

Grid Ref SN 850 146   OS Maps 1:50 000 sheet 160,
                                                 1:25 000   Brecon Beacons Western O/L

Altitude : 240 metres approx.

Length : 1000 metres approx.

Location   Both entrances to the cave lie at the rear of Rhongyr Isaf, on the right
at the bottom of the hill leading up to Penwyllt. At the rear of the garden, a stile on
the left leads to a group of dolines, one of which contains an entrance. However,
a second entrance, which lies at the rear of the garden and is surrounded by a
wooden fence, is the safer and more pleasant way in.
Description   A sporting but muddy cave which provides some variety from the
usual Swansea Valley caves.
The second entrance leads to an awkward drop through thin beds to a stream.
Downstream, the passage continues to a point where a crawl up on the right
leads to where a squeeze gives access to a larger section of stream passage.
This in turn can be followed to a traverse over a cascade and a wriggle down
over a pile of boulders into a small aven. An awkward rift out of the aven leads to
the head of Boulder Drop, a 10 m pitch best descended from the highest point of
the rift, rather than through the awkward squeeze in the floor of the rift. There are
not many good belay points around and a long length of rope is recommended
as a tether. The pitch is best descended using a ladder due to the friable nature
of the rock.
Most of the cave to this point is formed in a limestone shale and the rock is very
crumbly in places. However, the pitch lands in an impressive chamber enlarged
on a junction of joints, with the stream entering as a waterfall higher in the roof. At
this point solid limestone is encountered. The way on out of the chamber is to
follow the winding rift passage taking the stream. This is best done by starting in
the roof and alternating between different levels as the rift is tight and sinuous in
places. The passage continues for 750 m or so until a sump is reached. There is
only one significant inlet to this passage which is indicated by a trickle of water
entering the passage. An easy climb leads to a wide low bedding plane which
can be seen to continue for some distance.

Tackle   Boulder Drop - 10 m ladder, lifeline and long tether.
History   First recorded exploration by SWCC in 1950. Extended by cavers
working at Minerva Adventure Centre, then situated at Rhongyr Isaf, in 1985.

Pwll Dwfn   Grade 4

Grid Ref SN8340 1650   OS Maps 1:50 000 sheet 160,
                                                    1:25 000 Brecon Beacons Western O/L

Altitude: 399 metres

Vertcal Range : 93 metres

Location   The entrance is in the floor of the shallow valley which leads to the cliff
face above Dan-yr-Ogof and is best approached via the mineral track as
described for Tunnel Cave. It is about 650m back from the cliff face and a few
metres to the north of an old drovers track which crosses the valley. The entrance
is sometimes concealed by undergrowth especially in the summer.
Description   Pwll Dwfn is a vertical pothole with no significant side passages.
The water which runs in the bottom section of the cave has been traced to Dan-
yr-Ogof.
The entrance, which is just a hole in the floor of the valley, drops into a very short
section of passage leading directly to the first pitch. The pitch is only short and
there are good natural belays. From the foot of the ladder a short climb down
leads to a platform overlooking the second pitch. Belay ladder to rock and climb
down to the head of the third pitch. The third pitch is narrow and awkward but
there is a good natural belay. From the foot of the ladder a hole about 3m up on
the right-hand wall leads to the top of the fourth 'big' pitch. Belay ladder to
boulders. The pitch starts off narrow but gradually opens out. At the bottom, a
boulder strewn floor descends steeply to the last pitch. The pitch is usually wet
with a deep pool at the bottom which marks the end of the cave.
Tackle   1st Pitch – 6m ladder/rope, 8m belay and lifeline
                2nd Pitch – 15m ladder/rope, 8m belay and lifeline
                3rd Pitch – 9m ladder/rope, 8m belay and lifeline
                4th Pitch – 30m ladder/rope, 11m belay and lifeline
                1st Pitch – 6m ladder/rope, 8m belay and lifeline
                5th Pitch – 15m ladder/rope, 8m belay and lifeline
History   The cave was discovered in 1946 and first explored by S.W.C.C. in 1947.

Tunnel Cave   Grade 4
Alternative name: Cathedral Cave   1976

Grid Ref SN8388 1610   OS Maps: 1:50 000 sheet 160,
                                                    1:25 000 Brecon Beacons Western O/L

Length: 2135 metres+

Location   The cave has two entrances, the lower one being the show cave now
called Cathedral Cave which is close to Dan-yr-Ogof. The normal cavers'
entrance, Top Entrance, is reached by continuing past Dan-yr-Ogof on the main
road towards Sennybridge. At the point where the road crosses the River Haffes,

follow the river upstream to some sheep pens on the left. Just above the pens an old mineral track leads up the hillside. At the point where the track makes a couple of Z bends just below a small quarry, head for the high ground behind and to the left of the quarry. The entrance is situated on the high ground and is gated.

Access   The entrance is locked and the key is held by the South Wales Caving Club to whom application for access should be made. Access through the show cave can only be made in the company of a recognised leader.

Description   The cave is a system of high and narrow rift passages ending in the very large Davy Price's Hall which is now open to the public. Progress through the cave is mostly by climbing and traversing along different levels in the rift passages.

The entrance gate opens immediately onto a ladder pitch. Belay ladder to iron bar. At the bottom of the shaft a short climb down leads to another pitch. Belay to eyebolt on right-hand wall. The ladder lands on the 2nd Cascade which is a long dry calcite slope. *Upslope leads to a low connection to the Cascade Aven Extension, a complex series of passages which includes an awkward ladder pitch at the end of a crawl into the Courtyard.* Downslope leads to the Wire Traverse which is on the right-hand wall. *Straight ahead from the traverse is the Oasis* but the way on is down another, steeper, calcite slope – the 1st Cascade – with the help of a wire handline. *Part way down is the Balcony leading on the right to Balcony Passage*. Continuing the climb down the cascade on the left-hand side leads to Cascade Aven Chamber. A crawl straight ahead leads to climb down of 6m into a small chamber followed by another short climb down into a small chamber. A short section of passage then leads to an 8m climb down into the larger 5m Pot Chamber. *A floor level passage gives access to Marble Arch Passage via a squeeze through boulders,* while a climb up from the chamber leads to a sandy floored passage which leads to the narrower Wiggly Stal Passage. *A low opening in Wiggly Stal Passage leads to Pot Hole Passage which in turn leads via The Shute to the 35ft Pot Series.* Continuing down Wiggly Stal Passage the other end of Marble Arch Passage enters on the left. The passage continues for some distance to Saddle Corner. *By keeping low and to the right is the main route into the 35ft Pot Series which includes the large Waterfall Chamber.* By staying on a higher level and bearing round to the left the main passage continues and soon Cross Passage is passed on the left. A short distance past the entrance to Cross Passage is an awkward climb down to the Cross Joint. *The Cross Joint goes for short distance to the right where water enters and then sinks again at the foot of the climb.* A section of sandy floored passage is then followed by a smooth walled rift leading to the Junction. Bearing to the right the passage becomes wider and progress is made by climbing up and down boulders until the passage eventually emerges into Davy Price's Hall and the show cave.

EAST PASSAGE

The East Passage is entered by turning left at the Junction and leads via some steep upward slopes to a crawl over calcite. Cross Passage, which connects with the West Passage between the Cross Joint and Saddle Corner, enters from the left and soon after this junction the East Passage slopes downwards to a sandy floor. *After another 30m is the entrance to the passage, on the right, which leads via some crawls and a very shattered chamber to Xmas Grotto.* Continuing along the main passage leads to Steeple Aven Passage. Progress is mostly by scrambling over boulders, to Fork Junction. From here two ways on

The Time Machine, Daren Cilau
Streamway, Ogof Ffynnon Ddu 1

Bridge Cave, photo. by Tim Stratford

lead to Steeple Aven and the climb up into Sisyphean Chamber. From Steeple Aven a short climb leads to Switch-Back Passage which is narrow and involves a great deal of climbing up and down. This leads to a wider passage with a sandy floor and then another narrow section leads to the Final Chamber.

Tackle   Entrance Pitch – 12m ladder/rope and lifeline
            Second Pitch – 8m ladder/rope and lifeline
            Courtyard Pitch – 9m ladder/rope and lifeline

History   The cave was known as a small cave for many years but was extended almost to its present length in 1953 by members of the S.W.C.C. The cave was explored from the bottom upwards, the upper entrance being added later.
Survey: C.R.G. Publication No. 7 in 1958.

Upper Hospital Cave   Grade 3

Grid Ref SN8380 1510   OS Maps 1:50 000 sheet 160,
                                     1:25 000 Brecon Beacons Western O/L

Altitude: 322 metres

Length: 61 metres

Location   The cave is situated on Cribarth above Hospital Cave in a rock outcrop. The entrance arch can be easily seen from the road near Craig-y-Nos Castle (hospital).

Description   A small and uninspiring cave.
From the fairly large entrance the passage soon decreases in size to a crawl. At the end of this is a very tight squeeze followed by more crawling in a small passage.

Lesser Caves and Sites of Speleological Interest

Badger Hole SN844 156
Bloke's Dig SN837 167
Brick Works Quarry Cave SN855 153
Chas Jay's Dig SN9770 1649
Cribarth Sink SN833 143
Cribarth Slot SN831 145
Cwm Dwr Quarry Cave No. 1 SN8577 1564
Dai Hunt's Dig SN8740 1650
Engine House Dig SN8642 1613
Foxhole SN8527 1540
Gents Dig SN8586 1561
Gwyn Arms Rising SN846 166
Hospital Risings SN8920 1560
Hot Air Mine SN8661 1620
Ogof Coed Cae SN850 147
Ogof Dan Gam SN8093 1952
Ogof Ffordd SN8620 1590
Ogof Glan Byffre SN847 166
Ogof Nos Hir SN8634 1590

Ogof Tri Cam SN8050 1936
Ogof Twll Tal Ddraenen SN808 188
Ogof Un Cam SN8095 1936
Ogof-yr-Ardd SN850 146
Pant Mawr Sink SN8909 1622
Pentwyn Farm Resurgence SN8475 1442
Powell's Cave SN8498 1533
Pwll Byffre (OFD sink) SN8745 1660
Pwll Coediog Sink SN847 163
Pwll y Wydden Sing SN8305 1574
Step Cave SN837 162
The Chasms SN8793 1490
The Horseless Carriage Dig SN8561 1573
Weighbridge Quarry Cave SN8645 1625
Wern Pot SN865 160
Wheel Barrow Dig SN856 152
Whiskers Cave SN8514 1557
Whiskey Aven SN8509 1547

8. The Black Mountain

Dolphin's Pot   Grade 3

Grid Ref SN7621 1849   OS Maps 1:50000 sheet 160,
1:25000 Brecon Beacons Western O/L

Altitude: 558 metres

Length: 122 metres

Location   Situated in a shakehole on Foel Fraith a few hundred metres to the north of Pwll Swnd.
Description   The entrance leads to a chamber with a choice of three routes on, the lowest being a decorated bedding plane crawl. All three routes lead to a second lofty chamber. The cave ends at a boulder choke.
History   The cave was first explored by the S.W.C.C. in 1956 and extended in 1966.

Llygad Llwchwr   Grade 3

Grid Ref SN6690 1782   OS Maps 1:50000 sheet 159,
1:25000 Brecon Beacons Western O/L

Altitude: 229 metres

Length: 915 metres

Location   Situated about 2 km SW of the village of Trapp. It is marked on OS maps as the Source of Lougher. The cave should be approached from a small layby situated at SN672 177 on the small mountain road which skirts the western side of Banwen Gwythwch. Go through the gate and up the road for a short distance to a stile leading into the field on your left. Go over the stile and walk straight ahead keeping some large shakeholes to your left until you reach another stile and gate. On the other side a path leads around the fenced-off resurgence to a stile into the enclosure. The entrance to the cave is a small hole high up on the left of the resurgence.
Description   A fine river cave with a large series of upper level dry passages and four isolated river chambers separated from each other by long sections of totally submerged river passage. A considerable amount of water, which has been traced from near Herbert's Quarry some 8 km away, resurges from the cave. An awkward climb into the entrance leads to a dry crawl which after a short distance becomes a narrow rift. About 50-60 m from the entrance there are several small holes, on the left at floor level, which lead to the First River Chamber. Continuing along the main passage, via a boulder chamber, leads to the Parting of the Ways. Here, two small passages to the right lead to the Maze, a series of small rifts and tubes on different levels, and the Third River Chamber. To the left, a larger passage leads to the Second River Chamber via a short climb down from a balcony, best tackled on the left. On the opposite side of this chamber is an oxbow passage with a few small calcite formations, while downstream it is possible to climb up into an upper level tube which comes out in the roof of the First River Chamber via a tight squeeze.

THE BLACK MOUNTAIN

1. LLYGAD LLWCHWR
2. PAL Y CWRT
3. OGOF PASG-FOELWEN
4. OGOF DAN-Y-LLEAUD WEN
5. DOLPHINS POT
6. OGOF PWLL SWND
7. OGOF CARREG LEM
8. SINC Y GIEDD

LLANGADOG

A40

LLANDEILO

A483

1 ● ● 2

A4069

BRYNAMMAN

A474

AMMANFORD

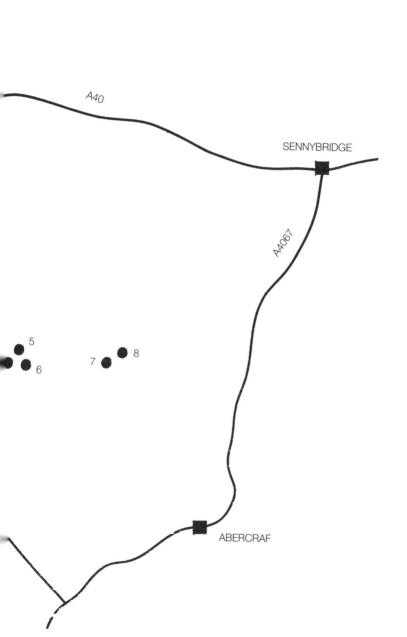

Continuing along the main passage from the Parting of the Ways, another passage on the right leads to a pitch into the Third River Chamber, while straight ahead leads to a slope down into the Fourth River Chamber.

THE UPSTREAM SUMP FROM THE FOURTH RIVER CHAMBER HAS BEEN PASSED BY DIVERS TO REACH CHAMBER 5 AFTER 76 M. AT A POINT 61 M FROM SUMP 4 BASE, THE RIGHT-HAND WALL TURNS THROUGH 90 DEGREES TO THE SOUTH AND BREAKS SURFACE AFTER 5 M IN CHAMBER 6. BEYOND, THE ROUTE CONTINUES UNDERWATER AND 46 M LATER THE PRESENT LIMIT OF EXPLORATION IS REACHED AT "THE SLOT".

Tackle   Third River Chamber - 4.5 m rope/ladder and 6 m belay.

History   First recorded exploration and survey by Thomas Jenkins in 1841.

WARNING   The water in the river chambers is normally deep in places.

Ogof Carreg Lem

Grade 4

Grid Ref SN8058 1804   OS Maps 1:50000 sheet 160,
1:25000 Brecon Beacons Western O/L

Length: 323 metres

Location   The entrance is a sinkhole situated to the west of Sinc y Geidd which is marked on OS maps.

Description   The entrance shaft is currently blocked due to a boulder collapse. The entrance leads to a small chamber and a wet shaft through boulders to a narrow vertical slot. This drops into a chamber 4.5 m wide and 2 m high where the stream sinks into boulders. *After a short distance, a passage on the left leads to the Left-Hand Series which can be followed for around a hundred metres.* The main passage is followed via a squeeze over a drop into a walkable passage going down dip. The passage continues in a southerly direction via two tight squeezes to the First Dig. This gives access to a bedding plane crawl which passes a large mud-filled chamber on the left called the Gadair Fawr. The passage continues via another squeeze and ends at a stal blockage. Just before this, on the right, is another passage leading to a dig.

History   First explored by S.W.C.C. in 1981. Line survey published in S.W.C.C.Newsletter No.97 (1983).

WARNING: THE CAVE IS LIABLE TO FLOOD. There are signs of severe flooding throughout the cave and there is probably no safe area to take refuge. The cave should therefore be avoided if there is any possibility of rain.

Ogof Dan-y-Lleuad Wen

Grade 3

Grid Ref SN7569 1851   OS Maps 1:50000 sheet 160,
1:25000 Brecon Beacons Western O/L

Altitude: 580 metres

Length: 215 metres approx.

Location   Situated in one of the many shakeholes on Foel Fraith to the northeast of Pwll Swnd.

Description   A short pot of about 4 m leads to a tight muddy slot. Beyond this the way on is a hands and knees crawl to the left, past a stalagmite in the middle

of the passage. After about 15 metres it is possible to stand up in a small chamber with large boulders at the head of a pitch. The 12 m pitch has clean fluted walls and lands on a descending boulder floor. The obvious way on is to the left of the pitch and almost immediately another passage is seen going off to the left. *This is Mark's Grotto, entered via a short climb and containing some nice formations but there is no way on. Care should be taken to avoid damaging the crystal floor.*
Continuing along the main passage, which runs up dip, the boulders eventually reach the roof and the way on is via an obvious passage to the right. Here there is a climb down over boulders and care should be taken as some of the boulders move! The passage reduces in size to around 3 m high and 2 m wide with a sandy floor and mud formations. After about 30 metres the passage divides with a 60 m long oxbow of large walking passage to the left. Part way along this passage is another short oxbow which has been taped off as it contains some fine mud formations, all of which can be easily seen from the main oxbow without crossing the tapes.
The main passage continues past the other end of the oxbow passage and via a traverse to an exposed climb down over boulders of about 3 m. *Between the two junctions with the oxbow is a small descending tube, to the left, which leads via an overhanging drop to the Lower Series. This passage goes to the left and right but ends in chokes in both directions, the southern choke having a voice connection with the upper series.* The 3 m climb brings you to the foot of a large boulder slope and the way on is up the slope and to the left, where the passage opens up with some fine calcite formations on the left. After a short distance, the passage veers to the left and another climb down leads to Canyon Passage, some 21 m high and 6 m wide. This leads after another 60 metres to an unstable boulder choke which completely blocks the passage. A small side passage has been followed for a further 60 metres.
Tackle   First Pitch - 12 m rope/ladder and lifeline
             Lower Series - 3 m rope/ladder useful for overhang
History   First explored by I.C.C. in 1991. Survey by I.C.C 1993, Descent (113).

Ogof Dan-yr-Odyn
                                          Grade 2

Grid Ref SN7160 1932   OS Maps 1:50000 sheet 160,
                                    1:25000 Brecon Beacons Western O/L

Altitude: 390 metres

Length: 60 metres approx.

Location   Situated to the south of a small road which runs west from the A4069 Brynamman to Llangadog road a kilometre or so northwest of Herbert's Quarry. The entrance is situated at the base of a small outcrop less than 100 metres from the road.
Description   A low entrance leads down over boulders and via a squeeze to a passage which is initially about 3 m high. The passage gradually loses height before reaching a group of calcite formations where great care is needed to avoid damage. The passage continues to a small chamber and a small gravel choke.
History   Explored by H.C.C.

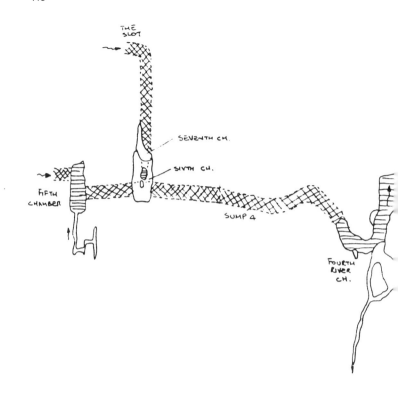

LLYGAD LLWCHWR

Plan based on TVCG/CDG surveys

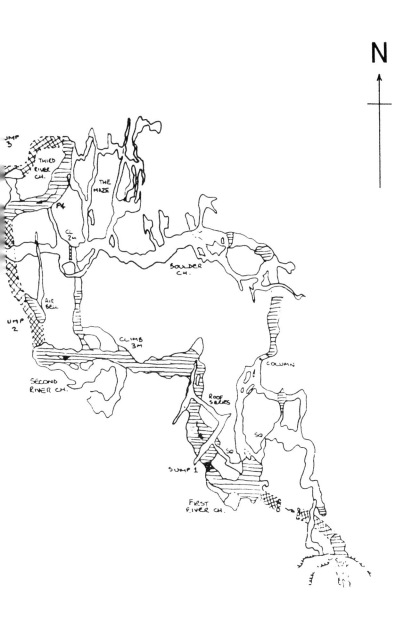

Ogof Diwedd-yr-Enfys   Grade 4

Grid Ref SN7870 1850   OS Maps 1:50000 sheet 160,
1:250000 Brecon Beacons Western O/L

Altitude: 411 metres approx.

Length: 304 metres approx.

Location   A difficult cave to find requiring a long walk over the moors. The entrance is situated on the eastern side of the Upper Twrch Valley.
Description   A small streamway leads for about 152 metres to a wide bedding plane which is low and wet followed by a tight duck. The stream soon disappears down narrow rifts and the passage continues as a dry sandy crawl. A small inlet enters from the right and two muddy squeezes are negotiated before the passage briefly opens up again. A small chamber can be seen beyond a too-tight squeeze but this has not been passed and does not look too promising.
Tackle   A wet suit is essential.
History   First recorded exploration by S.W.C.C. in 1981.
WARNING : THE CAVE IS LIABLE TO SEVERE FLOODING.

Ogof Pasg-Ogof Foel Fawr   Grade 3/4

Grid Ref SN7365 1881 / 7351 1873   OS Maps 1:50000 sheet 160,
1:25000 Brecon Beacons Western O/L

Altitude: 533 metres

Length: 834 metres

Location   The Ogof Pasg entrance is situated in Herbert's Quarry to the east of the A4069 Brynammon to Llangadog road. Follow the track to the top level of the quarry where it is split into two by a ridge. Level with the ridge is a shoulder between the two quarry faces. Climb up the shoulder, taking great care as it is very loose, and traverse around a ledge to the left about 21 m above the quarry floor. The entrance is situated at the end of the ledge and cannot be seen from the quarry floor.
The Foel Fawr entrance is less easy to find. It is situated on the western flank of Foel Fawr, about 400 metres from the quarry. By striking right before you enter the quarry the western facing slope is traversed just below the crest until the entrance is found in a hollow. It cannot be seen until you are almost on top of it.
Description   An interesting system formerly known as two separate caves. The connection between the two halves is via a very tight squeeze and not passable to anyone larger than average size. The description given is from the Ogof Pasg entrance.
Just inside the entrance the passage is 3.6 m wide and up to 3 m high and leads over calcited boulders to a sharp right turn. *There are two side passages on the left. The first is very narrow and mucky and can be followed for about 30 metres. The second is about 60 metres long and is walking size at first but soon lowers to a crawl which appears to end somewhere near the quarry face.* The main passage continues to the right with a nice level floor and much calcite on the walls. The passage then bears to the left and a boulder pile is met. The

passage continues below the boulders to a pool which sumps in wet weather but this can be avoided by climbing over the boulders to a sharp left turn where there are lots of straws on the ceiling. The passage then lowers to a crawl followed by an easy squeeze to the head of a sloping pitch.

A convenient stal is the only decent belay and a single rope or ladder with a long tether is sufficient to reach the bottom. From the foot of the ladder is a way back to the pool but in the other direction is a very fine canal passage, waist deep in water, which is followed for about 25 metres to a climb up a stal slope on the right. At the top of the slope there are two ways on. *To the right the passage can be followed for about 45 metres but again appears to end quite near the surface.* Straight on the passage becomes a low arch with a stal floor and the dried up remains of several crystal pools. The passage becomes progressively lower until it is a flat out crawl. This is followed by a short section of narrow walking passage and then another short crawl leads to a small chamber.

The passage continues via a dig through the stal floor to a very tight squeeze over a rock slab. *Beyond the squeeze and to the left is a small series of passages and a chamber.* To the right beyond the squeeze is a crawl via a couple of easy squeezes to a large passage which leads directly to the entrance of Ogof Foel Fawr. *To the right, just inside the entrance, is a hole and a difficult climb down into the Northern Passage. This passage starts off very high and narrow but the roof soon lowers as progress is made over boulders to a small shaft. This is free-climbable and the passage continues to another hole in the floor. There are passages above and below the hole but all become too narrow or are blocked.*

Tackle   Sump Bypass Pitch - 8 m rope/ladder, long tether and lifeline
          Northern Passage - 8 m rope useful for initial climb

History   Parts of the cave were explored in 1958 by S.W.C.C. Connection made and new survey drawn by H.C.C. in 1988.

Ogof Pwll Swnd   Grade 4

Grid Ref SN7622 1839   OS Maps 1:50000 sheet 160,
                                      1:25000 Brecon Beacons Western O/L

Altitude: 579 metres

Length: 915 metres approx.

Location   The cave is situated on the northeastern side of Foel Fraith and is best approached from Herbert's Quarry on a compass bearing of 112 degrees for a little over 3 km. The entrance which is in a short collapsed rift is marked by a cairn and is not too difficult to find in clear weather. The cave is marked on OS maps.

Description   The cave is a complex system of passages and chambers on various levels.

The entrance leads to a rift passage which becomes blocked after about 18 metres. A small passage to the left of the blockage then leads to the first pitch. Here, a short drop through a squeeze leads to the main part of the pitch which lands in a small chamber. A tube in the left-hand wall then leads to the main chamber. *To the left is the Old Series, a system of quite large passages and chambers ending at a boulder choke.* Straight ahead at the lowest part of the chamber is a small vertical tube which leads to the top of the second pitch. At the bottom of the pitch the passage leads over a hole in the floor to a small chamber. From here the two ways on rejoin again to continue to Shatter Corner. Here the passage takes a sharp left turn, past a cross passage, to a small hole in the left-hand wall. This hole leads to a tight crawl for about 30 metres to a junction with a larger passage. To the right soon closes down and the way on is to the left leading to the Wishing Well, a large blind pot. A rope descent part way down the pot leads to a small passage in the opposite wall. This passage leads to Five Ways Chamber. *To the right is the North Rift* while to the left two passages lead to Z Chamber. There are several routes leading off from Z Chamber. *To the right leads to a ladder pitch into a high rift - the West End. The most obvious passage straight on is South Passage ending after some distance at a run-in while a high level passage to the left leads to the Gallery.* Between South Passage and the Gallery is the steeply descending Lintel Passage which leads to Ringing Chamber. To the right of Ringing Chamber a small tube leads below boulders to the Last Pitch into the Basement. The cave ends at a large chamber blocked at the far end by a boulder choke.

Tackle   First Pitch - 9 m rope/ladder, belay and lifeline
          Second Pitch - 8 m rope/ladder, belay and lifeline
          Wishing Well - 8 m handline
          Basement Pitch - 15 m rope/ladder, belay and lifeline
          West End Pitch - 15 m rope/ladder, belay and lifeline
History   First explored in 1939. Major extensions made by H.C.C. in 1971. Survey by H.C.C. in 1973.

Ogof Tepod

Grade 3

Alternative Names: T Pot, Ogof Tepse

Grid Ref SN7620 1830   OS Maps 1:50000 sheet 160,
                              1:25000 Brecon Beacons Western O/L

Altitude: 563 metres

Length: 60 metres approx.

Location   Situated in a shakehole about 30 metres southwest of Ogof Pwll Swnd on Foel Fraith.

Description   A squeeze through boulders leads to a 15 m pitch in two sections which is best rigged from the surface. The second part of the pitch is a roomy shaft which lands in a walking size passage. This passage is well decorated and heads towards Pwll Swnd. The passage ends at a boulder choke which is believed to be very close to the entrance passage of Pwll Swnd.

Tackle   Entrance pitch - 15 m rope/ladder, tether and lifeline
History   Surveyed by H.C.C. in the late 1980's.

Pal-y-Cwrt

Grade 3

Grid Ref SN6734 1818   OS Maps 1:50000 sheet 159,
1:25000 Brecon Beacons Western O/L

Altitude: 277 metres

Length: 112 metres approx.

Location   A very difficult cave to find. From the Forge, which is about 2.5 km to the south of the village of Trapp, take the mountain road towards Brynammon. After about 800 m is a crossroads, turn left and follow the road to a bend where a track leads off to the left after a little over a kilometre and a half. The entrance to the cave is about 30 m east of the track and 100 m from the road.
Description   The entrance is just a hole in the ground which drops into the passage below. The passage descends quite steeply over boulders for some distance to a low chamber. There are two passages leading from the chamber but both become blocked with boulders within a short distance. An excavated hole in the left-hand passage however leads via squeezes to a tight duck which needs baling and then to a hands and knees crawl ending at a collapse.
History   Extended in 1980 by Teifi Valley C.C.

Sinc y Giedd

Grade 4

Grid Ref SN8101 1784   OS Maps 1:50000 sheet 160,
1:25000 Brecon Beacons Western O/L

Altitude: 434 metres

Length: 183 metres approx.

Location   Situated on the moors to the northwest of Dan-yr-Ogof and marked on OS maps.
Description   The cave is an active sink which periodically becomes blocked with stones and silt from winter flooding. The water resurges in Dan-yr-ogof. The climbable entrance shaft leads to a cave formed on three levels. From the middle section, a pitch of 13 m leads to the lower level which is heavily silted and contains a small stream. The downstream end of the passage has been periodically dug and would seem a good prospect for further discoveries.
Tackle   Pitch to Lower Level - 15 m rope/ladder, belay and lifeline
History   First explored by S.W.C.C. in 1947 and excavated periodically since then. Surveyed by S.W.C.C. in 1970.

Lesser Caves and Sites of Speleological Interest

Arm Pit   SN7511 1855
Arthurs Pot   SN7616 1811
Blaen-y-Cylchau Caves   SN761 188
Careg Cando   SN6550 1740
Careg Dwen   SN6590 1720
Careg Lwyd Cave   SN7358 1883
Carreg Cennan Caves   SN6679 1909

Carreg yr Ogof Caves   SN779 204
Carreg yr Ogof Sinks   SN780 216
Deadend Cave   SN7270 1930
Ffryd Las Resurgence   SN7739 1638
Ffydiau Twrch   SN7704 1623
Glyn Hir Cave   SN6415 1510
Guineas Cave   SN7472 1810
Llandyfan Church Resurgence   SN6477 1712
Lynfell Sink   SN7620 1750
Ogofau Foel Fraith   SN7610 1890
Ogofau Pen Rhiw   SN731 187
Ogof C Noddam   SN6836 1849
Ogof Creision   SN7282 1945
Ogof Dan-y-Chward   SN7368 1895
Ogof Edros Dros Pant y Ffynnon   SN7304 1908
Ogof Fern   SN7300 1910
Ogof Ger y Sarn   SN6761 1814
Ogof Myglyd   SN6418 1729
Ogof Pant y Dref Newydd Mawr   SN7271 1925
Ogof Pant y Ffynnon   SN7332 1903
Ogof Rhos Eilio   SN6865 1823
Ogof Tri Carn   SN8050 1936
Ogof Tro'r Gwew   SN7212 1932
Ogof Uwch y Ffordd   SN6838 1846
Ogof Uwch y Gorlan   SN6848 1855
Ogof Uwch y Gorlan Isaf   SN6848 1855
Ogof Will Fach   SN6418 1729
Ogof y Gigfran   SN7780 2126
Pwll Cwm Sych Sink   SN6907 1835
Pwll Cynrig   SN7824 2009
Pwll Foel Fraith   SN7612 1871
Pwll Pen Rhiw Wen Sink   SN7316 1855
Razor Pot   SN7613 1820
Redbrick Cave   SN7390 1890
Sinc Pant y Dref Newydd   SN7295 1938
Sinc-y-Pant   SN6770 1801
Upper Herbert's Quarry Cave   SN7366 1888
Waen Fignen Felen Sink   SN8260 1769

9. Gower

Bacon Hole
Grade 1

Grid Ref SS5610 8680   OS Maps 1:50 000 sheet 159,

1:25 000 sheet SS/58

Altitude: 10 metres

Length: 37 metres

Location   The cave is situated in the sea cliffs just to the west of Hunt's Bay and can be approached by the cliff path from Penard.
Description   An important bone cave which has produced the remains of a variety of animals including Straight-tusked Elephant, Soft-nosed Rhinoceros, Giant Ox, Bison, Reindeer, Wolf and Hyaena.
The entrance leads to a large chamber about 20m wide. There is the remains of an iron grill at the back of the cave.

Barlands Quarry Cave
Grade 4
Alternative name: Ogof Bishopston

Grid Ref SS5763 8959   OS Maps 1:50 000 sheet 159,

1:25 000 sheet SS/58

Altitude: 47 metres

Length: 457 metres

Location   The cave is situated to the northeast of Barlands Quarry which can be reached from the B4436 just outside Bishopston. A stream sinks in boulders and the entrance to the cave is about 5m above and to the side.
Description   An active system which takes considerable quantities of water at times.
The entrance leads directly to a tight ladder pitch. At the bottom of the pitch, a small chamber leads to two ways into the stream, both via squeezes. Following downstream the passage enters a chamber where the stream disappears but a crawl to the right leads back to the stream after about 30m. The stream is then followed along a narrow rift passage to a climb down into a chamber. The stream continues through the chamber to a duck and then Sump 1.
The sump can be bypassed by a 5m climb and then dropping back into the streamway on the other side. Downstream is another duck leading to a large chamber. On the other side of the chamber the stream continues through boulders to Sump 2. This has been passed to a small chamber.
Tackle   Entrance Pitch – 9m ladder, belay and lifeline.
Wet suit essential.
History   Major explorations made by C.C.G.
WARNING   The cave is liable to SEVERE FLOODING.

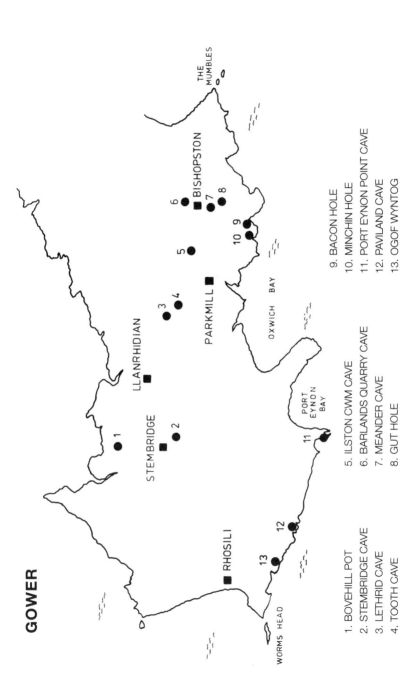

GOWER

THE MUMBLES

BISHOPSTON

LLANRHIDIAN

PARKMILL

STEMBRIDGE

RHOSILI

WORMS HEAD

OXWICH BAY

PORT EYNON BAY

1. BOVEHILL POT
2. STEMBRIDGE CAVE
3. LETHRID CAVE
4. TOOTH CAVE

5. ILSTON CWM CAVE
6. BARLANDS QUARRY CAVE
7. MEANDER CAVE
8. GUT HOLE

9. BACON HOLE
10. MINCHIN HOLE
11. PORT EYNON POINT CAVE
12. PAVILAND CAVE
13. OGOF WYNTOG

Bovehill Pot

Grade 3

Grid Ref SS4620 9360   OS Maps 1:50 000 sheet 159,

1:25 000 sheet SS/49

Altitude: 45 metres

Vertcal Range : 37 metres

Location   A difficult cave to find, it is situated in the cliffs near Bovehill Farm not far from Cheriton. The entrance is about 20m down the face and a handline is useful.

Description   Basically a vertical pot with very little horizontal development. The very low entrance slot leads to two successive pitches and the floor of a chamber. The sloping floor leads to a squeeze and then a scramble down into a second large chamber. At the bottom of the chamber is the third pitch through boulders to another chamber known as the Black Hole. From the floor of the Black Hole two pots can be descended, the deeper of the two ending in a pool.

Tackle   1st Pitch – 6m ladder, belay and lifeline
2nd Pitch – 6m ladder and lifeline
3rd Pitch – 8m ladder, belay and lifeline.

History   First recorded exploration in 1956.

Gut Hole

Grade 2

Alternative name: Guzzle Hole

Grid Ref SS5740 8860   OS Maps: 1:50 000 sheet 159,

1:25 000 sheet SS/58

Altitude: 15 metres

Length: 76 metres approx.

Location   Situated in the Bishopston Valley to the south of the village. The entrance is about 300m before the main resurgence of the Bishopston stream.

Description   A well known cave but of little interest to the sporting caver. The cave is on three levels. The lower large entrance leads to a stream which can be followed upstream to a sump. **THIS SUMP HAS BEEN EXPLORED BY DIVERS FOR A DISTANCE OF 37M.** A small hole on the left at the entrance leads to a low crawl which ends at another sump **WHICH HAS BEEN DIVED FOR 15M.** Another hole to the left outside the entrance leads to a crawl which becomes too tight.

Ilston Cwm Cave

Grade 1

Grid Ref SS5568 9025   OS Maps 1:50 000 sheet 159,

1:25 000 sheet SS/58

Altitude: 45 metres

Length: 60m metres approx.

Location   Situated in Ilston Cwm to the south of the village of Ilston near Parkmill. The large entrance can be easily seen on the southern side of the Cwm.

Description　The wide entrance chamber is soon choked to within a few inches of the roof by mud but an excavated tunnel through the mud leads to a crawl over boulders. Beyond the crawl the passage opens up and leads for a further 150ft. There are several choked side passages.

History　Known for a long time but extended to its present length in 1959.

Llethrid Swallet

Grade 4

Grd Ref SS5310 9120　OS Maps 1:50 000 sheet 159,

1:25 000 sheet SS/58

Altitude: 42 metres

Length: 610 metres approx.

Location　Take the B4271 Llanrhidian to Swansea road to Llethrid Bridge marked on OS maps, about 5km from Llanrhidian. A gate leads to a track running south to Green Cwm. After about 50m cut across to the right and climb over an old gate to the stream. The entrance is in the opposite bank.

Access　The entrance is gated and the key is held by the S.W.C.C. Apply to the Hon. Secretary.

Description　A well known cave which offers the most interesting trip on Gower. From the entrance a climb down through boulders leads to the stream. The first section of the cave is a crawl through boulders following the course of the stream. After some distance the stream flows through solid walls and a tight squeeze has to be negotiated. After about 200m the stream disappears and a climb up leads to a lofty chamber. An awkward, slippery climb immediately to the left then leads to a short section of passage which comes out by a large boulder into the Great Hall. This is a very large and impressive chamber which is finely decorated with a great number of formations both large and small. At the lowest point in the chamber a wide opening on the right leads to a mud bank where great care must be taken. Descend at the far right-hand side of the opening only. Cross over the bottom of the mud bank to a hole which leads down to a muddy passage and then drops into a continuation of the stream passage. In dry weather the passage can be followed via a mud chamber for about 120m to a sump.

THIS SUMP WHICH IS 2M LONG LEADS TO JUST 6M OF PASSAGE BEFORE THE NEXT SUMP IS MET. SUMP 2 IS 38M LONG AND 4.5M DEEP AND LEADS TO A FURTHER 18M OF PASSAGE AND SUMP 3 WHICH REMAINS UNEXPLORED.

History　The cave was first explored by S.W.C.C. in 1949.

WARNING　the cave is liable to SEVERE AND SUDDEN FLOODING and should not be entered in unsettled weather. The whole of the entrance series can flood to the roof and the water can back-up and flood a large part of the Great Hall.

Meander Cave

Grade 3

Grid Ref SS5741 8864   OS Maps 1:50 000 sheet 159,

1:25 000 sheet SS/58

Altitude: 13 metres

Length: 120 metres

Location   Situated in the Bishopston Valley about 33m downstream from Gut Hole. The entrance is on the right-hand side of a flood-channel which dries up in dry weather.
Description   The cave is only accessible in dry weather.
A drop down the side of the flood channel leads to an active stream passage. Upstream the passage quickly ends at a sump but way on is downstream to a duck. The duck leads to several more ducks and then the passage divides into two. Both passages can be followed until they join up again a little way before the final sump.
THE SUMP HAS BEEN EXPLORED BY DIVERS TO A POINT WHERE THE PASSAGE CLOSES DOWN AFTER 7M AT A DEPTH OF 4.5M.
Tackle   A wet suit is essential.
History   The cave was first explored by members of the C.C.G. in 1974.
WARNING   The cave is liable to SEVERE FLOODING.

Minchin Hole

Grade 1

Grid Ref SS5550 8680   OS Maps 1:500 000 sheet 159,

1:25 000 sheet SS/58

Altitude: 6 metres

Length: 46 metres

Location   Situated in the sea cliffs and can be reached by walking eastward along the shore from Foxhole Bay. The entrance is in a large fissure.
Description The largest of the Gower bone caves. Finds include the remains of Reindeer, Bear, Wolf, Hyaena, Bison, Lion, Soft-nosed Rhinoceros, and straight-tusked Elephant. Evidence has also been found of human habitation. The cave is a large single chamber about 21m high.

Ogof Wyntog

Grade 2

Grid Ref SS4340 8640   OS Maps 1:50 000 sheet 159,

1:25 000 sheet SS/48

Altitude: 9 metres

Length: 74 metres

Location   Situated at the Knave which is along the coast to the east of Mewslade bay. A footpath leads from the car park near the main road to the Knave. The entrance is in the western corner of the bay above a small rising.
Description   A double entrance leads to a low squeeze. Beyond the squeeze is

a comfortable size passage. After a few feet a side passage to the left leads to a hole overlooking a sea cave. Continuing along the main passage leads to a small chamber. To the right a sandy passage leads to a sand choke. Straight ahead a climb down over a stal bank leads to the main sea cave.

Paviland Cave   Grade 1
Alternative name: Red Lady Cave, Goats Hole

Grid Ref SS4370 8590   OS Maps 1:50 000 sheet 159,

1:25 000 sheet SS/48

Alternative: 9 metres

Length: 22 metres

Location   From Pilton Green on the Swansea to Rhosili road a footpath leads to the clifftops and a deep valley. Follow the valley to the bottom and scramble over the rocks to the sea's edge. The cave can then be seen in the cliff face to the west. Access at high tide is dangerous.
Description   The cave is of great archaeological importance and has been excavated many times. It was inhabited by early man and finds include a partial human skeleton, flint flakes, a carved ivory pendant and ring, and bone needles. The cave extends for about 22m and is about 4.5m high. There is a climb on the right leading to a higher entrance.
History   First recorded exploration in 1822. Important archaeological finds include the famous 'Red Lady of Paviland' made by the Rev. W. Buckland.

Port Eynon Point Cave   Grade 1

Grid Ref SS4680 8440   OS Maps 1:50 000 sheet 159,

1:25 000 sheet SS/48

Altitude: 6 metres

Length: 22 metres

Location   The cave lies at the southern tip of Port Eynon Point. It can be approached by following the shore from the village at low tide. Access to the cave at high tide is dangerous.
Description   The cave has been excavated and the remains of Lion, Bear, Woolly Rhinioceros, Mammoth and Red Deer have been found.
The entrance is large but the passage becomes narrower and lower further in.

Stembridge Cave

Grade 3

Grid Ref SS4680 9190   OS Maps 1:50 000 sheet 159,

1:25 000 sheet SS/49

Altitude: 45 metres

Length: 76 metres

Location   The cave is situated in the back garden of a cottage. From Stembridge take the road towards Old Walls for about 400m. The cottage is then on the left-hand side of the road.
Access   Ask permission at the cottage.
Description   The entrance leads over a rubbish heap to a walking size passage. After a short distance is a crawl. A left turn part way along the crawl leads to a climb down through boulders to a small chamber. To the right of the chamber a ladder pitch leads to a lofty passage which is followed to a boulder pile. There are several side passages and the boulder pile can be climbed to a small passage with some formations.
Tackle   8m ladder, belay and lifeline.
History   The cave was first explored in 1939 and extended in 1957.

Tooth Cave

Grade 4

Grid Ref SS5320 9110   OS Map 1:50 000 sheet 159,

1:25 000 sheet SS/58

Altitude: 50 metres

Length: 1525 metres

Location   The cave is situated in Green Cwm about 100m south of Lethrid Cave. Follow the track beyond the second gate and then turn up through the trees to the left. The entrance is in a small cliff and has an old gate on it.
Access   The cave is gated and the key is held by S.W.C.C. Apply to the Hon. Secretary.
Description   Gower's longest cave comprising of a series of low crawls and a larger and more lengthy Main Stream Passage.
From the entrance a narrow passage leads to a gate and a squeeze into a narrow rift. The rift drops quickly and a rope is needed for the final drop into Bone Chamber. The chamber is very well decorated with some fine curtains and has been excavated, yielding evidence of human habitation. To the right a narrow passage leads to another small chamber with a boulder floor. A squeeze down through boulders at the far side of the chamber leads to a low crawl and short section of rift passage. Beyond the rift the passage decreases in size again at the start of a long section of low crawls. *There are two ways into Razor Passage on the left which can be followed for over sixty metres* but the way on is to bear right. After a further 15–18m a short climb down leads to a continuing and slightly larger passage. The passage can be followed for some distance until it becomes too tight but a decorated crawl on the left is the way on. The crawl is followed to a junction where two ways lead on to the main Streamway. One, a muddy crawl to the right, the other, a very low crawl straight ahead. The Main Streamway is

fairly large but also quite low in places. Following the Streamway to the right leads through some fine, almost circular, clean phreatic passages. *There are several small side passages which all close down within a short distance.* The passage ends at a climb down to a clear static sump.

In the other direction, the main Stream Passage can be followed over much stream debris for a considerable distance to a boulder pile. *A climb up through the boulders leads to an aven and then another climb into the small Aven Series.* Beyond the boulder pile the Main Stream Passage continues to a sump. In very dry weather this sump dries up and it is possible to continue to several decorated chambers and eventually the terminal sump.

History   The cave was first explored by the S.W.C.C. in 1961.

WARNING   The cave is liable to SEVERE AND SUDDEN FLOODING and should not be entered in unsettled weather.

Lesser Caves and Sites of Speleological Interest

Barlands Quarry Sink   SS5766 8963
Bishopston Sink   SS5760 8920
Bishopston Valley Rising   SS5745 8839
Bosco's Den   SS559 868
Bowens Parlour   SS557 868
Burry Head Rising   SS4568 9028
Caswell Bay Cave   SS5916 8765
Caswell Bay West Rising   SS5898 8895
Caswell Bay East Rising   SS5923 8762
Caswell Valley Sink   SS5960 8876
Cathole   SS538 900
Crawley Rocks Cavern   SS520 879
Crowhole   SS558 869
Culver Hole   SS406 930
Culver Hole   (Port Eynon)
Cwm Ivy Tor Cave   SS4350 9408
Daw Cave   SS5757 8912
Deborah's Hole   SS434 863
Decoy Pond Sink   SS5190 9090
Devil's Kitchen   SS547 873
Forrester's Cave   SS551 872
Hills Orchard Cave   SS4337 9367
Holywell Rising   SS4970 8990
Inner Sound Cave   SS631 873
Kettle Collapse   SS5751 8913
Kitchen Well   SS5390 8960
Kittle Hill Cave   SS576 890
Leason Well   SS4831 9280
Leathers Hole   SS530 877
Llanrhidian Rising   SS4960 9220
Llwyn y Bwch Swallet   SS483 915
Longhole   SS452 851
Lower Daw Pit Sink   SS5750 8909
Mewslade Cave   SS423 873

Mewslade Quarry Cave   SS423 975
Moor Mills Sink   SS5050 9124
Murton Stream Sink   SS5880 8895
Newton Stream Sink   SS5896 8874
Newton Cave   SS454 882
North Hill Tor   SS453 938
Old Quarry Pot   SS4957 9215
Ogof Canddo   SS5751 8898
Ogof Ci Coch   SS5751 8897
Ogof Hentecil   SS5751 8915
Ogof Rhosilli   SS406 878
Parc le Breos Sink   SS5300 8940
Ravenscliff Cave   SS546 872
Red Chamber   SS426 868
Scree Cave   SS5746 8843
Spritsail Tor Cave   SS4256 9371
Stoneyford Sink   SS4940 9150
Southall Cave   SS476 892
Thurba Head Cave   SS423 873
Well Head Rising   SS5392 8970
Widegate Rising   SS5670 8790
Worms Head Cave   SS394 877

10. West Wales

Carregwylan Cave Grade 1

Grid Ref SN1050 4580   OS Maps 1:50000 sheet 145, 1:25000 sheet SN/14

Altitude: 0 metres

Length: 61 metres

Location   The cave is situated in the sea cliffs near Carregwylan a short distance from Moylgrove,Cardigan. The entrance is at sea level and can only be approached at low tide.
Description   The large entrance leads to a roomy passage about 3 m x 3 m and then to a large chamber about 9 m high with a cross passage to left and right.
History   First recorded exploration in 1958.

Cathedral Cave Grade 1

Grid Ref SN1300 9688   OS Maps 1:50000 sheet 158, 1:25000 sheet SN/19

Altitude: 0 metres

Length: 215 metres

Location   Situated at sea level near Sandy Bay on Caldey Island, about 3.5 km to the south of Tenby.
Description   A large sea cave with four entrances. The most easterly of the entrances is 15 m wide and 20 m high but the passage size diminishes towards the back of the cave.
History   This is a well known cave which has undoubtedly been known for centuries. Surveyed in 1990 by Keith Jones.

Crwbin Cave Grade 3

Grid Ref SN4688 1292   OS Maps 1:50000 sheet 159, 1:25000 sheet SN/41

Altitude : 180 metres

Length : 183 metres

Location   Situated in a quarry near the village of Crwbin. Turn left off the Llanelli to Carmarthan road in the middle of the village and follow the narrow road downhill. Where the road levels out at the valley bottom is an overgrown quarry on the left of the road and there is a small area to park a car. The remains of an old tramroad can be followed uphill from here to a point where it becomes obscure and overgrown. Bear right into the quarry and ascend a little to a sloping bench with a small bare rock face. The entrance to the cave is in this bench and is easily seen.
Description   The small entrance leads through a crawl to a more roomy descending rift passage. This main passage then continues for some distance but it can sump in one place after heavy rain. There are a few side passages but all end within a short distance.
History   First recorded exploration by SWCC in 1952.

WEST WALES

1. CARREGWYLAN CAVE
2. GREENBRIDGE CAVE
3. OGOF CAPEL DDYGEN
4. CRWBIN CAVE
5. OGOF PANT-Y-LLYN
6. OGOF GLAN GWENLAIS
7. OGOF NANT HYFRYD

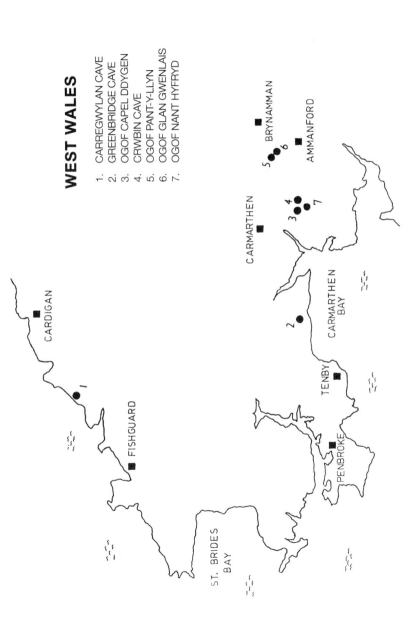

Greenbridge Cave

Grade 3

Grid Ref SN2260 0920   OS Maps 1;50000 sheet 158, 1:25000 sheet SN/20

Altitude : 70 metres

Length : 97 metres

Location   Situated to the northwest of Pendine. Follow the road past the Green Bridge Inn to where the stream sinks on the right-hand side of the road. The entrance to the cave is at the sink.

Description   The large entrance leads to a low stream passage and then a lofty chamber. Beyond the chamber, the stream passage continues but gradually decreases in size and becomes very muddy. Eventually the roof comes down to meet the water. There are a few small side passages but all close down within a few metres.

History   The first recorded exploration was by SWCC in 1957.

Ogof Capel Ddygen

Grade 2

Grid Ref SN4670 1280   OS Maps 1:50000 sheet 159, 1:25000 sheet SN/41

Altitude : 164 metres

Length : 146 metres

Location   Situated in the same quarry workings as Crwbin Cave. From Pontyberem on the Llanelli to Carmarthan road, follow the road up the hill towards Carmarthan. On reaching the village of Crwbin take the small road on the left just a few metres past the village sign and in front of a bus shelter. Follow this road to a junction with another small road on the right and then follow this down a steep hill. At the bottom, the road bears around to the right and the ruins of an old chapel (Capel Ddygen) covered in ivy can be seen in the field on the left-hand side of the road. Immediately opposite the ruins a rough track on the right leads into a quarry. Follow the track bearing left, past the first two faces, and then scramble up a grass bank on the right to a small terrace. In front of you is a clump of bushes and trees and the entrance to the cave is behind this under a wide overhang.

Description   The walk-in entrance is situated at one end of the overhang and leads into a large chamber. A large passage with calcited walls leads off to the left of the chamber but ends disappointingly after 20 m or so at a mud run-in. To the right just inside the entrance is a small passage which leads to a short climb down a pot to a descending passage. At the bottom is a small chamber which fills with water in wet weather. It is sometimes possible to continue along a low bedding crawl in water to 76 m of muddy rifts ending at a sandy dig. However, this extension quickly fills with water after only slight rain and can remain flooded for many months.

History   First explored by SWCC in 1951 and surveyed in 1956. Extended in 1987 by Teifi Valley C.C.

Ogof Carmel

Grid Ref SN4982 1640   OS Maps 1:50000 sheet 159, 1:25000 sheet SN/41

Length: 100 metres approx.

Location   Situated in a quarry about 500 metres west of the village of Carmel.
Description   The entrance leads to a descending passage down a calcite slope with some totem pole type stals. A short constricted passage then leads to a 12 m pitch into a chamber with two ways on. *One passage leads back up dip towards the quarry face.* The other is a muddy grovel, 3 m long, to another chamber which is 12 m high and 9 m wide. A climb over boulders that span a rift passage leads after about 30 metres to a small chamber with a number of passages leading off. All these passages end within 30 metres or less.
Tackle   12 m ladder, belay and lifeline
History   Explored by Croydon C.C. in 1976.

Ogof Glan Gwenlais

Grid Ref SN6050 1620   OS Maps 1:50000 sheet 159, 1:25000 sheet SN/61

Length : 190 metres approx.

Location   The cave is situated in the Glan Gwenlais quarry to the NW of Llandybie. From Ammanford, take the A483 towards Llandeilo and after passing through Llandybie a side road on the left is signposted to Pentre Gwenlais. Follow this road up the hill and through the village. A junction is reached after about 1.5 km with some old quarry buildings straight in front of you. The quarry is behind these buildings and the entrance to the cave is 9 m above the quarry floor on the left. It requires an awkward climb up and a bolt already situated in the wall may be a useful aid but should not be relied upon.
Access   Cavers are advised not to visit this cave at present as there is a dispute between local people and conservationists with the owners of the quarry who want to re-open it to extract the limestone. Visits to the cave will only exasperate the situation.
Description   An unpleasant cave due to its restricted nature and fragile rock. It should not be underestimated because of its short length.
A stooping size entrance leads to a sandy, mud floored passage which soon descends to a flat-out crawl in mud through a narrow passage to a small, heavily silted chamber. The obvious way on is under a low arch into a larger passage where hands and knees crawling eventually gives way to a walking size phreatic passage. This passage then narrows temporarily but larger passage is soon regained. After 40 m the passage divides. *To the left soon closes down* but to the right a rift passage is followed until it becomes too narrow. A difficult climb up through this passage allows access to a wider rift passage which leads to a small collapse of boulders obstructing the passage below. To the left access is gained to a narrow meandering passage which leads to an area of boulder collapse where one can stand up. A short and unpleasant section of passage containing sharp and jagged rock is then encountered, followed by a very narrow passage which allows only gradual movement sideways. After 10 m the roof lowers and the passage becomes too constricted but a small passage to the left leads to a large phreatic passage.

To the left, the phreatic passage can be followed for a short distance until the roof lowers to form a low arch. A squeeze, negotiated on one's back, then allows access to a narrow but tall chamber with no obvious way on. To the right, a collapsed section of rift passage is encountered with recently fractured rock hanging precariously from its walls. A short climb up between the boulders leads to the continuation of the passage and then a short climb down reaches a boulder strewn passage of standing height. Loose rock is a constant problem and 20 m later a short climb up leads to a narrow rift passage. Traversing a hole in the floor, a further collapsed section of larger rift is encountered. *A narrow climb down leads to the lower continuation of this passage but becomes too tight after 12 m.* A climb up leads to a higher continuation of the same passage which is in a very unstable condition. A squeeze around precariously positioned boulders is then negotiated and the passage continues small and uncomfortable over small boulder collapses. After 25 m solid rock is regained and the roof suddenly descends to a small mud floored passage which soon ends at a calcited boulder choke. This is the present limit of exploration but the passage can be seen to continue and there is a strong draught.

History   First explored by ICC in 1985. Survey by ICC.

WARNING THE CAVE IS LIABLE TO FLOOD. The narrow descending passage just after the entrance can sump in wet weather. Parts of the cave are also VERY UNSTABLE with many lose boulders.

Ogof Gofan   Grade 3

Grid Ref SR9590 9296   OS Maps 1:50000 sheet 158, 1:25000 sheet SR/99

Altitude : 12 metres

Length : 125 metres approx.

Location   Situated in sea cliffs on Saddle Head, Pembroke and not easy to find. It is reached by ladder or rope from the top of the cliff.

Description   Although relatively short, this cave is very well decorated and has been protected from vandals by its location and difficult access. Archaeological remains have been found in the cave.

There are two entrances in the cliff connected by a crawl. From the larger entrance a crawl leads to a passage which is quite well decorated and then to a large chamber which is decorated with some fine calcite formations including some excellent columns. There is a pool on the bottom of the chamber.

A passage continues from the chamber for a further 50 metres and again contains many calcite decorations.

Tackle   Pitch to entrance - 15 m ladder or rope

History   First explored in 1968.

Ogof Nant Hyfryd   Grade 3

Grid Ref SN479 133   OS Maps 1:50000 sheet 159, 1:25000 sheet SN/41

Length : 300 metres approx.

Location   Situated in the same quarry as Crwbin Cave and Ogof Capel Ddygen, near the village of Crwbin. The entrance is in the face about 17 m above an intermediate bench.

Description   A single joint controlled passage which carries a small stream in wet weather.
The large entrance passage quickly ends at a very narrow passage going left and right. The way on is to the right where the passage is initially partially obstructed by shattered rock. As progress is made away from the quarry face the passage becomes stable and is typically elliptical in shape with a trench along the floor. There are also a number of small, well preserved, calcite formations. There are several squeezes along the way passing boulders and formations. The passage eventually ends at a boulder choke.
History   First recorded exploration in 1989. Survey by C.Smith.

Ogof Pant-y-Llyn   Grade 3

Grid Ref SN6050 1670 OS Maps 1:50000 sheet 159, 1:25000 sheet SN/61	

Altitude : 210 metres

Length : 284 metres

Location   The cave is situated in an old quarry known locally as Craig Derwyddon which is to the NW of Llandybie behind the Glan Gwenlais quarry. From the junction opposite Glan Gwenlais quarry entrance, turn right and follow the road for a few hundred metres, past a lake on the left. At the far end of the lake an old quarry track leads up through the trees. At a junction with another path turn right and enter the quarry. There were originally two entrances to the cave but the way through the lower, larger entrance, has now collapsed. The other entrance known as Ogof Craig Derwyddon is situated about 5 m above the larger and more obvious entrance.
Access   The same situation as that which applies to Ogof Glan Gwenlais effects this cave and cavers are advised to avoid the area at present.
Description   An interesting cave that is formed in very steeply angled limestone beds which are well exposed in the Glan Gwenlais quarry immediately behind Craig Derwyddon.
The entrance leads via an excavated crawl to the large Main Chamber which has a steep floor of boulders and mud. Some of the boulders are loose and so care must be taken. Going downslope to the bottom of the chamber leads to a tight descending bedding plane and then a tiny chamber. From here a steep muddy tube descends to a junction. An awkward climb down on the left leads to a large chamber and the collapsed route to the other entrance while to the right a passage descends past some gour pools to where it divides into two ascending passages. Both of these passages end quickly but the floor of the passage prior to where it divides contains several holes which lead to a bedding plane chamber connecting with the large chamber below the collapsed choke.
Back in the Main Chamber, near the top on the left-hand side, is a sloping bedding plane which is well decorated. The taped-off path should be followed to avoid damage to the formations. The bedding plane develops into a fine and steeply descending phreatic passage, Totem Passage, eventually leading to a large chamber with a small stream. *To the right leads to a small grotto and then to a pool with a constricted duck on the far side. The passage can be seen to continue but access is at present impossible.* Crossing the stream chamber to the left, the stream flows under a low arch and a wet squeeze beyond gives

OGOF PANT-Y-LLYN

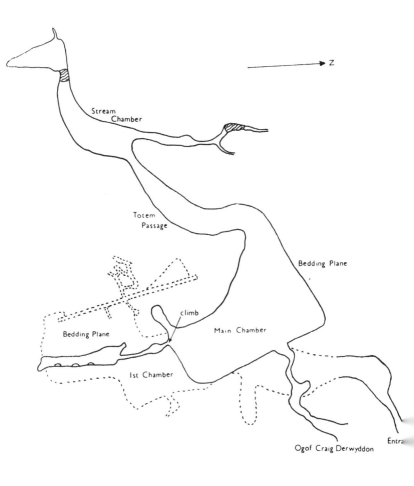

based on survey by I.C.C.

access to the final chamber. The stream can silt up the squeeze and it may be necessary to dig it out.

History   The entrance has been known for some time. Major extensions in 1983 by CCC and ICC.

WARNING   There is a seasonal danger of CO_2 build-up in Ogof Craig Derwydden, particularly when the entrance crawl is dry.

Smugglers Cave   Grade 1

Grid Ref SR0876 9448   OS Maps 1:50000 sheet 158, 1:25000 sheet SR/09

Altitude : 0 metres

Length: 90 metres

Location   Situated at the eastern end of the "Bay of Caves "at Lydstep, about 5 km south-west of Tenby.

Description   A large sea cave with three entrances which is well known locally.

History   Surveyed by Keith Jones in 1986.

Lesser Caves and Sites of Speleological Interest

Capel Dyddgen Resurgence   SN4606 1233
Capel Hirbach Resurgence   SN5292 1472
Carmel Caves   SN595 162
Coygan Cave   SN285 093
Craig Llygad Resurgence   SN4910 1410
Cwar-y-pistyll   SN6240 1670
Daylight Rock Fissures   SS1498 9659
Gorswen Quarry Caves   SN577 160
Hoyle's Mouth Cave   SN111 003
Huntsmans Leap Cave   SR9646 9284
Little Hoyle Cave   SS1116 9995
Merlin's Cave   SN1360 0030
Mynyddygarreg Cave   SN4410 0920
Nanna's Cave   SS1458 9697
Ogofau Hengoed   SN4470 1025
Ogof Cil yr Ychen   SN6143 1643 (site only)
Ogof Garreg Wen   SN2125 0955
Ogof Isel   SN591 162
Ogof Morfan   SR9452 9490
Ogof Pen Cyfrwy   SR9586 9287
Ogof Rhidian   SN604 165   Rogwen Point Resurgence SN223 075
Ogof Serth   SN5088 1445   Seal Cave   SS1336 9617
Ogof Uchel   SN591 162   Sinc Ger y Ffordd   SN3170 1892
Ogof Wen   SN5118 1450   Skull Cave   SS1471 9688
Ogof-y-Cae   SN4570 1325 (site only)   Stackpole Head Pothole SR9930 9430
Ogof-y-Dinas   SN6120 1660   Stalactite Cave   SS1430 9707
Ogof yr Ychen   SS1464 9693   Star Rock Cave   SR9779 9380
Ogof y Wern   SN5200 1385   St.Sampson's Cave   SS1434 9709
Potter's Cave   SS1434 9709   Waterfall Cave   SN2294 0758

Welsh Glossary

Aber	mouth (river)
Afon	river
Agen Allwedd	keyhole
Allt	wooded hillside
Ar	on
Araf	slow
Bach	small
Bryn	hill
Buwch	cow
Bwa	bow
Bwoch	goat
Bwlch	pass; saddle of a hill
Bychan	small
Byr	short
Cae	field
Cadno	fox
Canol	middle
Capel	chapel
Carreg	stone
Cartref	home
Castell	castle
Ceffyl	horse
Cefn	back; ridge of a hill
Chwarel	quarry
Chwith	left
Ci	dog
Cil	recess
Clogwyn	cliff
Coed	wood
Coeden	tree
Cor	dwarf
Cornel	corner
Cors	bog
Crawnon	pus; matter; treasure
Cwm	valley
Cymer	confluence; junction
Cynnes	warm
Craig	rock
Clwb	club
Da	good
Dafad	sheep
Dan	under

Du or Ddu	black
Dewi	David
Dim	none
Dinas	city; fortress
Dol	meadow
Dringo	to climb
Dryw	wren
Dwfn	deep
Dwr	water
Dwy	two
Dydd	day
Dyn	man
Dynes	woman
Eglwys	church
Eira	snow
Enw	name
Eryr	eagle
Esgyrrn	bone
Fechan	small; little
Fferm	farm
Ffordd	way; ford
Ffrydiau	fountains
Ffrynau	ovens; well
Ffynnon	spring; well
Fignen Felen	yellow bog
Fraith	speckled
Gaeaf	winter
Gaer	camp
Gam	crooked
Gnau	nuts
Glan	river bank
Glas	blue
Glyn	valley
Gor-	over
Gor	pus; matter
Gwaen	rough grazing
Gwal	wall; lair
Gwlad	country
Gwlyb	wet
Gwylan	seagull
Gwyn	white
Gwynt	wind
Hafn	gorge; hollow
Haul	sun
Hen	old

Heol	road
Hir	long
Isaf	lower
Isel	low
Llan	church
Llawer	many
Lle	place; room
Lleuad	moon
Lliw	colour
Lliwiog	colourful
Llwyn	grove
Llwynog	fox
Llygad	eye
Llyn	lake
Maen	standing stone
Maes	field
Mawr (fawr)	big
Meirw (marw)	dead
Mochyn	pig
Moel	bald, bare hill
Mur	wall
Mynach	monk
Myndd	mountain
Nant	stream; brook
Neis	nice
Nesaf	next
Neuadd	hall
Newydd	new
O	from
Ochr	side
O Flaen	in front of; before
Ogof	cave
Ogofeidd	caving
Onnen	ashtree
Pant	valley; hollow
Pen	head; top
Pentref	village
Perllan	orchard
Parc	park
Perthi	bush

Plas	place; large house
Poeth	hot
Pont (bont)	bridge
Porth	haven; gate
Pwll	pool; pit
Rhaff	rope
Rhiw	hill
Rhyd	ford
Robin Goch	robin
Serth	steep
Shon (Sion)	John
Siambr	chamber
Silff	shelf
Siom	disappointment
Sir	county; shire
Swnd	sand
Sychbant	dry valley
Sychrhyd	dry ford
Tal	tall
Tan	under; fire
Tarddiad	source; origin
Tir	land
Tlws	pretty
Tawel	quiet
Tref	town
Tros	over
Twll	hole
Twm	Tom
Ty	house
Uchaf	upper
Urchel	high
Wen	white
Wern	pasture; meadow
Wyntog	windy
Y or Yr	the
Yn	in
Yn fawr	much
Yns	island
Yohen	oxen
Ysgol	school
Ystrad	road

Index